SEE THESE BANNERS GO

THE STORY OF THE
PROTESTANT CHURCHES IN AMERICA

by

FRANK S. MEAD

Author of *The March of Eleven Men*

THE BOBBS-MERRILL COMPANY
Publishers

INDIANAPOLIS   NEW YORK

FIRST EDITION

PRINTED AND BOUND BY
BRAUNWORTH & CO., INC.
BOOK MANUFACTURERS
BROOKLYN, NEW YORK

To
MY FATHER
GOOD CHURCHMAN
AND BETTER CHRISTIAN

CONTENTS

FOREWORD

LIKE a mighty army they swept across the seas in the wake of Frobisher and Drake: Anglicans and Puritans from near Bow-bells or Oxford town; Pilgrims, from Leyden; Scotch Presbyterians from Aberdeen and Irish from the Emerald Isle; Calvinists and Lutherans from Scandinavia and Amsterdam; Quakers, Baptists, Methodists, Seceders whom the frontier transformed to Campbellites. Protestants all! They swarmed into the New-World forests, building a church for God wherever the frontiersman built a town, planting the banners of Christ their Royal Master along the road as the course of empire westward took its way. They sowed the seeds of modern education, built our first schools and colleges; their religious ideals became the ideals of our politics and government, produced the Declaration of Independence and begat American democracy; their constancy and courage are become the most admirable traits of our national character, the warp and woof of our lives.

Crowns and thrones have perished, kingdoms risen and waned, but their Church of Christ still holds the highest hill in every American town. We shall never move out of its shadow, never shake off the Puritan, never see die in our blood the strain of the rebel dissenter, never escape the impact of the Calvinist temper. The mark of the Protestant pioneer is on us, in us. He has captured our nation, molded it slowly, surely, into the mightiest Christian nation on the globe. We who tread its soil are treading where the saints have trod, following where they led, where Chaplain Whitaker baptized Pocahontas and Elder Brewster preached, where Roger Williams suffered and Francis Asbury rode the long, long road, where Penn sat with the Indians under Shacka-maxon's elm and Alexander Campbell ranged the old frontier, where . . .

THE EPISCOPALIANS

SEE THESE BANNERS GO

CHAPTER I

THE EPISCOPALIANS

PROTESTANTISM came to these United States on the decks of a pirate ship; it came ashore in 1579 with buccaneer Sir Francis Drake, son of a British clergyman and scourge of the Spanish Main. Drake knelt on a California beach with his chaplain, Francis Fletcher, to plant the cross and pray a prayer and claim the new land for England's Virgin Queen. Swords of Elizabeth and the cross of Christ. A pirate and a priest!

An odd pair, these two. One was building England's navy, England's empire on the seas, announcing a new era with the throaty thunder of his salty guns. Humble Chaplain Fletcher was doing more than that. He was, like Drake, a prophet of dim days yet to come; he was the forefather, pioneer, of a new church just then rocking in the cradle of mother-Church-of-England, to be known years hence as the Protestant Episcopal Church in the United States. He was also a link to dim ages gone; he was a priest of the old Church of England.

Just how old that is, we dare not say. Ask the

scholars, the historians. Some will say that this has been the Church of England ever since that day in 597 when Augustine, the Roman missionary-monk, landed on the shores of Kent; that, strengthened by the isolation of its island home, it has always been peculiarly English in its customs and practices and never quite Roman or Roman Catholic. Others will say that it was born with the coming of Henry VIII, who "made England Protestant that he might divorce one woman and marry another." Take your choice. There is truth in both positions. Possibly, Henry didn't found the Church of England, possibly he just found it; possibly, all he did was to cast off officially the yoke of Papal captivity and lead his people back to the ways and customs of a church created and evolving long before the popes were ever thought of. Possibly, he did nothing of the sort. It matters little now, except that this Church of England was the mother-church from whose ancient bosom came our Episcopalians, who, for a century and a half, in America, still bore the name of the Church of England.

It was old and it was strong. Strong with a strength born of struggle for its life, of being tossed about on the waves of religious warfare as fiercely as the ships of Drake were tossed about in the cradle of the deep. It was buffeted, hard, in the days of confusion following Henry's official break with Rome, when persecution drew a deep red scar from Bournemouth to Berwickupon-Tweed. The Catholics and the Protestants were fighting it out; monasteries were pillaged and destroyed, nunneries were sacked and burned; Sir Thomas More defended Rome and lost his head for it, and a new (Protestant) Ten Articles of Religion were drummed into the heads of England's youth while the clergy squabbled over the elements of the Supper, over forms of worship and the Mass. Then Henry died, leaving behind him a church freed from Rome but chained to the State, an Established Church, with King instead of Pope for Protector. As a liberator he was splendid, but in joining Church and State he repeated one of the saddest mistakes in history.

After him came Edward VI, who gave us two Books of Common Prayer and Forty-two Articles of Religion; then that Bloody, Catholic Mary who discarded Protestant rituals and brought back the Mass, who cast out the Prayer Book for Latin liturgy and holy water, who forced a Parliament to its knees before a Roman cardinal and who burned a host of Protestants at the stake; after her, Elizabeth, spinster, redheaded, touchy, Protestant, with her Drake.

Elizabeth fixed her eye on America's shore and pushed her ships across the foam to seize and settle and hold it for the Crown. She sent forth brave colonists who were brave in vain; sending them into the New-World forest was like transplanting tropical orchids in Labrador.

They wilted, died, vanished, almost before the ships that brought them had sailed home again.   Sir Humphrey Gilbert tried it twice; twice, it was disaster.   Undaunted, the Queen granted a charter to pipe-smoking, cloak-throwing Sir Walter Raleigh; his colony disappeared, without a trace, like thin smoke in a tempest, but not before their chaplain (a priest of the Church of England) had baptized Manateo the Indian and baby Virginia Dare, the first converted Indian and the first child born of English parents in America.   Virginia perished with the colony, Manateo went back to his redskin god, and the dark forest waited in grim silence for more Englishmen to come.   More came.   Captain John Smith came, in helmet and buckler, slashing a clearing in the startled forest with his bright sword, clearing the ground for the first permanent settlement. At his side was Robert Hunt, clergyman.   It was 1607.

"We did hang an awning (which is an old saile)," wrote Captain John, "to three or four trees. . . ."   And under the awning, between the elms, they built a rustic altar.   With fallen trees for kneeling benches, they read with Robert Hunt from King Edward's *Book of Common Prayer*, "Spare thou those, O God, who confess their faults.   Restore thou those who are penitent; according to thy promises. . . ."   Discordant sounds, for the air of the forest primeval; sounds of foolishness, outlandish, alien, to the savages staring from the bush at this minister come with his worshipers to build a nation where their tepees stood.

More colonists came and with them more ministers. There was Master Burke and Alexander Whitaker, "Apostle to the Indians," who gained fame by baptizing Pocahontas. Ere long a House of Burgesses, the first legislative body on the new shores, was meeting in the chancel of the Jamestown Church, settling the salary of Virginia's clergymen at "1500 pounds of tobacco and sixteen barrels of corn." (State and Church were united here, as in England. It was an Established Church all over again.) It was not a very attractive salary; it attracted a poor type of minister. Some came who could "babble in the Pulpit and roar in the tavern," who were better at hunting foxes than at feeding their sheep. A visitor wrote to the Bishop of London (who paid very little attention to his colonial church), "It would . . . make the ears of a sober heathen tingle to hear the stories that were told me of several clergymen. . . ."

But they were not all like that. They couldn't have been, for as the Church spread over Maryland, New England, New York, New Jersey and the Carolinas, it gradually became the social and spiritual center of community life. A steady quiet growth set in, in which the emotional fickleness of the new frontier was challenged by cold reason and out of which developed a church noted as a conservative force for righteousness.

Through the doors of this transplanted church came the finest people in the colonies, to sit with commoners who were getting the feel of equality for the first time in their lives. Ladies in satin sat in quaint box pews, fighting off the cold with fur muff and foot warmer; proud plantation gentlemen and New York merchant princes, sons of the cavaliers, sat stiffly, proudly, thinking perhaps as much of cotton and tobacco as of prayer. (Cotton and tobacco were important, at that. When a Virginia divine urged Attorney General Seymour to remember that the people of Virginia had souls to be saved, Seymour replied, "Souls! Damn your souls. Make tobacco.") In the rear galleries sat the slaves and on the wall was the royal coat-of-arms. It was a pleasant picture, a solidly established, conservative, blue-blooded church. The picture was shattered and the solid walls rocked the night a young man in Boston glanced over his shoulder at two lanterns hung in the belfry of Old North Church and galloped off toward Concord.

The Revolution almost destroyed the colonial Church of England, along with the government back home. Remember, these clergymen were appointed in England, sent out from England, paid from England; remember, for years the Church and State had been one; remember, each clergyman in America, on ordination, had taken an oath of allegiance to the King. That made many of them Tories. In the North, with few exceptions, the clergy were Loyalists. In New York alone forty thousand Tories joined the King's forces, while thousands more fled to Canada. Those who stayed at their posts paid a fearful toll. They were imprisoned and flogged and dragged through the streets; their estates were confiscated and their churches closed or turned into stables for rebel cavalry. But many of them went Continental. Rector William White was chaplain of Congress for years; Reverend Charles Thurston was a rebel Colonel. In the pews of the church sat great patriot-laymen: Washington, Jefferson, Patrick Henry, John Jay, Robert Morris, John Marshall, two Lees, John Randolph. In a fair census, we should find more patriots than loyalists.

The presence of Tory and patriot on the same kneeling bench tells the story: divided, the house fell. When Cornwallis gave up at Yorktown, his falling sword severed the last connecting bond with the Church of England. Now the Americans had an English Church cut off from England; an Episcopal Church (the word Episcopal means "governed by bishops") without a bishop; a Christian Church with a handful of bewildered ministers, a divided laity and an oversupply of wrecked or broken churches. Extinction was just around the corner. But thanks to that stubborn Anglican sense of loyalty which has always marked the Episcopalian, the corner was never turned.

Reverend James J. Wilmer arose in a conference in Maryland to propose that "the Church of England as heretofore known in the province be now called *The Protestant Episcopal Church.*" The name caught on in other provinces, and soon the whole American Church had adopted it. That settled the separation issue. Reverend Samuel Seabury journeyed from Connecticut to Scotland, to a little upper room in Aberdeen, where three bishops laid their hands upon his head and made him a bishop; he came home to lay his hands upon another American head; shortly, there was a bishop for every colony. That settled the Episcopacy issue. The Church of England soon approved of every move; reaching hands across the sea, Briton and Yankee forgot Lexington and Yorktown and faced the future together. Therein lies the strength of the Protestant Episcopal Church; through its heart runs a silver cord of patient understanding which refuses to snap, a dogged devotion to its major task which will not be put aside. The Episcopalians have "stickability"; in the years since the Revolution, while sister-denominations have suffered split after split, this Church has had but one. The Reformed Episcopal Church broke away in 1873 and today has fewer than nine thousand members.

After Yorktown there were happier, smoother seas. Great teachers, preachers came to show the way. Bishop Griswold swept across New England, driving down

Episcopalian foundation stones in the face of Puritan prejudice and making himself beloved as he did it. John Henry Hobart, student, thinker, man of affairs, fathered the famous General Seminary in New York, baptized eighty-nine Indians at one service and ninety-seven at another. Philander Chase and James Harvey Otey rode as God's horsemen in the West, rode daringly into the brawling log-cabin towns and camps of the frontier, prayer book in one hand and six-shooter in the other. (Otey, once, thrust his great bronzed fist under the nose of a pugnacious gambler and said evenly, "Before you try to throw me out of the window, feel that.") Schools, hospitals, mission stations and churches went up as the Indian fell back. The church of kings and cavaliers was digging in, facing a new order and a new kind of man and winning, slowly, for a God as old as time.

Then hot shot fell on Sumter and the Civil War was on. Would disruption, division, come again, as it had in '76? It seemed inevitable in '61. New England rectors were abolitionists and a southern bishop (Polk) became a general under Lee. Other churches split over slavery; the Methodists and Baptists and Presbyterians saw their houses split into northern and southern divisions and to this day (why?) have not been able to forget the war and join again. But the Episcopalians never let that happen. They simply separated for the moment, as two travelers might separate to walk around a mud puddle in their road and join again when the obstacle was passed. The name of every absent southern bishop was called in the New York Convention of 1862; northern churchmen corresponded with southern all through the war; Bishop McIlvaine of Ohio and fighting Bishop Polk of Louisiana prayed for each other by name, in their chancels, every Sabbath day. There was no antagonism, no hatred; there was only sorrow and sympathy. And when the last rattle of musketry died out at Appomattox and Yank and Johnnie Reb went home to the spring plowing, the southerners came quickly through the door left wide open by the northerners and it was a *national* church once more. Again, they had survived the minor tempest of politics.

From Appomattox to now, they have strengthened their lines and perfected their organization. As the nation proceeded to build a representative democracy under a flexible Constitution, the Episcopalians proceeded to build a representative, democratic form of church government under a flexible ecclesiastical code. More than any other, the government of this Church parallels the government of the United States. The local unit is the parish (corresponding to the municipality) governed by local rector and vestry. Then comes the diocese, which is composed of groups of parishes (as the county is composed of groups of towns), each presided over by a bishop but governed largely by the laymen, as the state is presided over by the governor but controlled by its citizens. Once in three years there is a General Convention, composed of an upper House of Bishops and a (lower) House of Clerical and Lay Deputies (the Senate and the "House," the House of Lords and the House of Commons). The Convention governs through a National Council.

Under this plan they moved out to the attack; their strategy has always been to conform to the course of battle, to extend their lines as emergencies arose. To meet the rise of the new learning and rationalism, they have built five colleges and fifteen seminaries and a string of famous "preps." (They have always been educators; among the first colleges in America were old Henrico, old William and Mary in Virginia.) To meet the rise of labor and aid in labor's struggle for justice they created a Church Association for the Advancement of the Interests of Labor. (Only last year one of their rectors went riding in a Paterson Black Maria in defense of labor's right to strike and picket.) To meet the rise of the liberated Negro they have built ten Negro schools in Dixie; to minister to the vanishing Indian they have developed the finest Indian missions in America; to care for sailors ashore in seaport towns they have a dozen Seamen's Institutes; in the late fight to protect America's childhood from filthy motion pictures, their venerable weekly, *The Churchman,* led the way.   And the 1934 General Convention seconded the efforts of *The Church- man* by urging federal control of the whole motion- picture industry.

The Episcopalians have built the most beautiful churches and cathedrals in the United States, tributes to the medieval masters of the Gothic arch and to the art of the modern architect.   They have filled these churches with nearly two million communicants.   Ask any one of these two million what he believes and he will point you to two creeds: The Apostles' and the Nicene.   He believes in the Apostles' Creed, he says, because it is wide enough to let anyone in and keep no- body out; he believes in the Creed of Nicea because he thinks it is the ideal statement of Christian faith.   They contain, he says, all that is necessary, essential and per- manent.   He believes thoroughly in God the Father and Christ the Son, in sin's forgiveness and in the resurrec- tion of the dead.   He says, "These things are essential. The rest?   Well, we leave you free to think that out for yourself."   His creeds are not clubs, not iron rods to enforce conformity; his Thirty-Nine Articles (based on the Augsburg Confession and the old Forty-Two Articles) are not clubs either; they are more for informa- tion than for required acceptance.   File this in one of your memory's pigeonholes: *no church in America is so intellectually hospitable as the Protestant Episcopal;*

*in no other communion is there such room for variation,
individuality, independent thinking and religious liberty.*
No priest is ever told, "You must preach this;" no layman has belief thrust upon him. This Church prefers
to emphasize great principles and to leave its communicants free to think on all else.

As it is with the Episcopalian's Creeds, so is it with
his sacraments. He has two sacraments: Baptism, and
the Supper of the Lord. If he desires he may be immersed; if he does not wish immersion, he may be baptized by pouring. When he takes the Supper, he may
take it from a table or from an altar, sometimes by day-
light and sometimes by candlelight; now there are
flowers, now none; one rector may read the prayers,
another intone them. It is your choice, yours to take
as you wish.

Some Episcopalians are High-churchmen, with an
abundance of ritual and ceremony and an eye on Rome,
and some are Low-churchmen, with a minimum of ritual
and ceremony and much evangelical, almost Methodist,
zeal. Some are Broad-churchmen, including both High
and Low, both ritualists and evangelists. Modernists
and Fundamentalists may be happy here, or anyone between them; Anglo-Catholics and anti-Catholics may
worship, do worship, side by side, may read from their
Book of Common Prayer the *General* Confession, or
the prayer of St. Chrysostom: "Almighty God, who

hast given us grace at this time *with one accord* to make our common supplication unto thee . . . "

The *Book of Common Prayer!* That is glorious. It is a growth, a depository, a treasure-house of the faith of the ages, with its roots deep in the devotions of old Israel. Its order of morning and evening prayer was born in the Old Testament synagogue; it has the words of Christ and the Apostles; it has the glory that was the Greek Testament, the grandeur that was in the ancient Latin Christian, the cries of the martyrs in old Rome. It echoes the language of the days of chivalry, the tongues of monks and popes and perfect, gentle knights; it resounds with the exultant cries of the Old-World discoverers who found new worlds across the seas and new heavens beyond the stars. It is second, in its lilting cadence, only to the King James version of the Bible, and it is the priceless gift of the Episcopalian to the Christian world.

This is not, in numbers, the largest church in the United States. It will never be that, for it takes a type of mind to be Episcopalian, a type of heart to appreciate its historic beauty and its future mission. Only he will be happy here who can revere the truth for which the fathers of this Church have struggled since Christ and who will seek earnestly, tolerantly, the new truth which God is constantly pouring on the world.

THE CONGREGATIONALISTS

Chapter II

THE CONGREGATIONALISTS

IN THE red whirl of any revolution there are always three species of rebel: there is a conservative, a middle-of-the-roader, and a rabid radical. These three always manage to be on hand when trouble comes to town; they hooted at the tumbrils in the French Revolution; they fought over tea and taxes in 1776; they were in Richmond in '61. And when the revolution which was the Reformation arrived in Merrie England, the same jolly three were in the saddle and ready to go.

The conservative was the Anglican. He wanted revolution, but not too much; he held the torch gingerly; he would keep his old Church sans Pope and all things papal.

The middle-of-the-roader was the Puritan, who went further than the Anglican. He would try to reform the National Church with the help of the national authority; he wanted to choose his own leaders and pray his own prayers, but he did *not* want to leave the Church of England.

Then there was the radical, the left-winger, the "red," the Separatist. "The old Church?" said he. "It's hopeless. Out with it. Down with it. We'll have our own. We'll break clean, separate ourselves...." Good Englishmen hated them, dubbed them variously Separatists, nonconformists, Brownists, Congregationalists. What's in a name? By *any* name, they were still a stench in the nostrils of orthodoxy.

The men who settled Virginia were Anglicans; they transplanted an Established Church.

The colonists who came to Massachusetts Bay in the Great Migration of 1630-40 were Puritans, who wanted a reformed church.

The Pilgrims who came to Plymouth were Separatists, Congregationalists, left-wingers with a still unconquered thirst for freedom in their bones, objectors who have never yet been satisfied with their condition or the condition of their world, plungers who have laughed at obstacles and hunted frontiers, who have built a church that has made faith an adventure and not a creed.

John Wyclif was their grandfather; their father was Robert Browne. Wyclif and his Lollards started them on their half mad and holy career by telling them that the Bible and not the Pope was their real authority and guide. Browne, in 1581, wrote a little tract which was to become the Magna Charta of Congregationalism. He called it *Reformation Without Tarying for Anie*. He'd tarry for nobody, said Robert Browne, he'd wait for no slow reformers to bore from within. He'd take his religious marching-orders from no king, no queen, no bishop. Were there bishops in Galilee? Did Christ bow the knee to Cæsar? He did not; neither would Robert Browne. He called upon all who loved the Lord to come out and be separate from England's bishop-ridden, royalty-ruled Church, to establish a true church, a "company of redeemed believers, joined in covenant," which was the only church worthy of the name. He was hounded all over England for saying that, hounded over to Holland. In his later days he repented and returned to the old fold; he was buried, like John Wesley, in the robes of a priest of the Church of England.

But a mighty army of those who had absorbed his poison did not come back. Pursued and harried by the King's horses, whipped and pilloried by the King's men, hosts of them shook the dust of England from their feet and scurried, like Browne, to Holland. A little group of worshipers from Scrooby did that; they fled first to Amsterdam, then to Leyden, where they stayed twelve years. William Brewster, postmaster on the Scrooby road, was with them, and preacher John Robinson, who told them once that "God hath more Truth and Light yet to break out of His Holy Word." William Bradford, seventeen, was a silk-dyer's apprentice; young Miles Standish was a British soldier, Samuel Fuller a doctor. They were pilgrims, they thought, on the hunt for truth and light.

Holland was a haven and the Dutch were kind, but pilgrims are by nature restless. They wanted something Holland could not give: a church of their own, in a commonwealth of their own, on soil of their own. Hence, one bright morning in 1620, they packed the last of their babies and Bibles and bric-a-brac aboard a tiny craft, the *Mayflower,* and dropped down over the horizon. Fools. Fanatics. They'd never make it. They'd be back, like Robert Browne, broken, penitent.

They made it. Their shell of a ship groaned in the sea, the main beam buckled and deck gear was torn away by waves as high as mountains and tempests howled through the rigging while women clutched their children in wild-eyed fear, but they made it. One day in November a sailor aloft cried out, "Land ho!" It was Cape Cod. The day after New Year's Day they found the spot they wanted and went ashore with ax and adz to build nineteen log houses along a single street. At the head of the street, atop a hill, they threw up a great house which overawed the rest: it was a fort, a church, a storehouse. Every Sunday they marched up the hill to church. To a Congregational Church, a church sans bishop, sans king, sans ancient prayer book, sans everything but a doughty courage which thrived on death and hardship and an ideal of liberty which was to fashion a republic, a nation which was to carry on its coins a typically Pilgrim motto: "In God We Trust."

Ere long, death was riding down their main street on a phantom runaway, snatching a fearful toll from every cabin door; within a year, half of them were dead and buried in the middle of the road. Over their graves, come Sunday, the whole town marched, on their way to worship God in the hilltop church. The Indians mustn't know where those graves were. It took men (and women) with Pilgrim iron in their blood to do that. They had it. When the *Mayflower* sailed away to England the next April, there was not a soul aboard her save the crew. The fifty-one survivors stood on the bleak hill and watched her go.

(Fireside critics and smug historians point with pride to the foolishness they find in the Pilgrim. He was narrow, they say, intolerant, bigoted. Maybe so. But we should place more credence in their arguments if we could see *them* tramp over the graves of their babies and their wives to morning prayer, or stand on some bleak hill and watch *their Mayflower* go; we should like to see *them* leave their firesides and face death, cold, hunger, loneliness, for the sake of *their* ideal.)

Meanwhile, the Puritans who had tarried in England were standing with their backs to the wall. James the First and his archbishop, Laud, were driving them hard, slitting their noses and branding their cheeks and cutting off their ears. In 1628, John Endicott led the first Puritan refugees to Massachusetts Bay; in 1630 a thousand came, in seventeen ships. By 1640, no less than twenty thousand of England's finest and most cultured Puritan citizens were settled in Charlestown, Salem, Watertown, Roxbury, Malden, right next door to the despised Separatists at Plymouth! That was like putting two strange wildcats together in the same cage; it meant trouble. Puritan and Separatist within a stone's throw of each other and plenty of stones to throw.

But none was ever thrown. God or destiny reached down to stir their fantastic broth with the ladle of common pain. A plague of sickness broke out among the Puritans; they ran short of medicines and they had no doctor. Up the coast went deacon-doctor Samuel Fuller, Pilgrim, to bring back many from the gates of death, to pray at the biers of the dead when he lost them. When his work was done and the plague stayed, Salem's Governor Endicott wrote Plymouth's Governor Bradford: "I acknowledge myself bound to you for your kind love and care in sending Mr. Fuller among us, and I rejoice that I am by him satisfied regarding your judgment of the outward form of God's worship. . . ." And that was going far, for Endicott.

Their mutual suspicions had been dissolved in Doctor Fuller's medicines. Gone were their English-bred differences, gone the threat of a divided church on the new shore. One touch of suffering had turned New England Congregationalist. Within a decade there were thirty-three churches there and thirty-one of them were one hundred per cent Congregationalist.

They had their own church now, in which they could govern themselves, worship when and where and as their consciences commanded. And they proposed to keep it. That's what they had come over here for. Did you think the Pilgrims and the Puritans came to establish religious freedom? Not they. They came to get that freedom for themselves, and with it once clutched in their fists they were determined to hold it against all comers. Roger Williams challenged it and he was exiled; Anne Hutchinson held objectionist prayer meetings in her parlor and found herself cast out; Quakers were flogged and banished and twenty witches died in Salem in 1692. Only church members could vote or hold office; taxes supported the Congregational Church. It was a closed corporation and a strict one; the Congregationalists were determined to carry out their own religious notions, undisturbed. "All familists, Antinomians, Anabaptists, and other Enthusiasts shall have free liberty to keep away from us," wrote one of them. They kept too many away; they exiled too many; they needed men like Roger Williams and Thomas Hooker.

Hooker! A leader of men was Thomas Hooker. He preached a reckless sermon on the lack of true democracy in Massachusetts. Among other things he said, "The fountain of authority is laid in the free consent of the people. . . . The choice of the magistrates belongs to the people. . . . The people . . . have the right to set the bounds and limitations of the power and place of those who are called."

The people, the people, the people! Of the people, by the people, for the people. That was being preached by a Congregational preacher generations before Abraham Lincoln was born. The Puritans liked sermons, but they didn't like that one. Out went Thomas Hooker with a little company of disciples, to the green Valley of the Connecticut, to found the First Church of Hartford, to found a state named after the river, to stand for a political philosophy which makes him the father of his country in a sense that George Washington never was. Says historian John Fiske: "The government of the United States today is in lineal descent more nearly related to that of Connecticut than to any other of the thirteen colonies. . . . The Constitution of Connecticut marked the beginning of American democracy, of which Thomas Hooker deserves more than any other to be called the father." Score another for the Separatist!

By 1700 there were one hundred and thirty Congregational Churches in New England. They looked healthy, but they were not. The stiff spine of the Puritan had held his head a bit too high, made him too exclusive for his own good; his stiff gospel was unattractive. There had been trouble with the Indians, argument over policies of Church and government. The old united front was cracking; decline was setting in; the Church was losing ground and influence. Compromises didn't help: the suffrage was extended, the system of taxing everybody for the support of the Church abolished, religious freedom extended and a Half-Way Covenant by which the children of baptized parents were admitted to Church membership was tried. But the trouble lay at the heart of Puritanism, not on the surface. Thousands were nominal church members; thousands more turned their backs on it completely. Enthusiasm waned. The old emotion was dying. Something had to happen, and it happened.

A young man began preaching at Northampton. He was Jonathan Edwards, a graduate of Yale at seventeen and one of the greatest minds ever to blossom on American soil. He spent thirteen hours a day in his study, studying Calvinism. Appalled at the stagnancy of religion and the decline of morals, he began preaching an enlarged, modified Calvinism which warmed the hearts of his hearers. He preached that justification was by faith alone; that salvation was God's gift; he dangled the sinners of Northampton over the brimstone of hell and he slapped the old Puritan conscience awake. He called them back. Repent ye!

Northampton repented. New England repented. Across the colonies rolled a tidal wave of religious enthusiasm. When Edwards was nearly spent, there came George Whitefield from England, a tavern-keeper's son and a product of Oxford's Holy Club, to preach in the fields and on courthouse steps and to stir the rising generation of ministers to revivalistic efforts undreamed of ten years before. Men stood in line, with lanterns, before dawn, at the doors of the church; thousands came back; thousands came in. It was the Great Awakening. The whole countryside was ablaze with God.

Like a fire in an old tenement, its results were good and bad. Princeton was founded; a new and enlightened New England theology was under way; the warmth of new faith replaced the frigid air of carelessness and men of nobler character sat in the seats of government; above all, the nation was strengthened for the bitter test of the Revolutionary War, a war largely inspired by the teachings of freedom and liberty thundered long from the pulpits of the Congregationalists. If ever a church cradled a rebellion, the Congregationalists cradled the Revolution. They came through it unscathed, for they were solidly American. There was no chance for a split among those who had rebelled in England, years before.

But there were destructive results following the Awakening, too. The revivalists who went in for the teaching and methods of Edwards and Whitefield came to be known as the "New Lights"; it was they who founded Princeton. Those who disapproved of them and their methods were the "Old Lights." Rival schools of preachers fell to competing with each other; between the two was a great gulf soon fixed, a gulf to be widened beyond hope of bridging when the Unitarians left the Congregationalists in the opening days of the nineteenth century.

That Unitarian split is one of the queerest and most regrettable schisms that ever divided the forces of American Protestantism. Queer, is it not, that a church as liberal and adaptable as the Congregationalist would be rocked by doctrinal disputes? Regrettable, in that a new view of Christ's divinity, with its attendant corollaries of sin and salvation, heaven and hell, could tear away from them all but two of their churches in Boston and their finest college, Harvard.

A split like that would wreck many a church, but not the church of the frontier-hunting Pilgrim. What happened now reminds us of what happened when Marshal Foch wrote that immortal message from the front: "My left is crushed, my center is falling back. I am attacking with my right." In the very midst of the Unitarian conflict, with their own house afire and facing ruin, a handful of Congregationalist college boys decided to . . . attack with their right! They looked out beyond the clouds of conflict, out across the Alleghenies and the Rockies and they said, "We'll go there." They looked across the seas at China, Burma, India, Japan and they

said, "We'll even go there!"　And there they went, in
the most audacious missionary adventure known to history.　Right at the moment when the graybeards were
shaking their heads over the state of the Church, a
phalanx of mere boys set in motion forces which created
the American foreign missions enterprise, which forced
the organization of the first home missionary societies
in the United States.　They burst the bounds of old New
England, hunting new frontiers.　It was a mad
maneuver.　It won.

Foreign missions had a lowly beginning in our country;
foreign missions began in a haystack.　In a haystack and
a shower.　Four students of Williams College banded
themselves together in a wild dream.　They vowed they
would send a "mission or missions to the heathen."　They
met one day in a grove, to pray for it.　God drove them
into a haystack with a shower.　That Haystack Prayer
Meeting gave the world the Haystack Volunteers.　They
prayed about it and they took off their coats: by 1810
there was an American Board of Commissioners for
Foreign Missions.　Out to the Orient, under their aus-
pices, went Adoniram Judson, Gordon Hall, Samuel
Newell, Samuel Nott, Luther Rice, in the advance guard.
The Puritans had begun to backtrack across the seas:
swiftly, they occupied Hawaii, Turkey, China, Japan,
India, Mexico, the islands of the Pacific.　An endless
stream of preachers, teachers, doctors, farmers, put their

hands beneath the elbows of their brothers everywhere, to lift them toward their places in the sun. The end is not yet. The job has only begun. Go anywhere and you'll stumble over a Congregational missionary.

While these were in the rifle pits of the far-flung battle line others were working at home. As early as 1793, nine preachers from Vermont, New Hampshire and New York were out on the western frontier; every state in New England had organized a home missionary society before the opening gun of the War of 1812. Ahead of them all ran Manasseh Cutler, Congregational minister and veteran of the Revolution. Cutler had an idea: he considered the thousands of acres in the Northwest Territory and he considered the thousands of veterans of the Revolution and he considered bringing them together. He told Congress that and after typical Congressional delay, Congress said, "Go ahead. We'll furnish the land; you settle it." Out of New England, at the call of Manasseh Cutler, went the "Ohio Company," with their wagon trains and their muskets and their Bibles, on the way to add another empire to the United States. They sailed down the Ohio in a craft they called the *Mayflower!* Cutler was careful. He got Congress to pass an ordinance that no person in the new Territory should ever be molested "on account of his mode of worship or religious sentiment," that schools should be built and that slavery should be forever prohibited! Thus was slavery barred from Ohio, Indiana, Illinois, Michigan and Wisconsin, by a Congregational parson! Daniel Webster said of Cutler's Ordinance of 1781 that no other single law of any single lawgiver, ancient or modern, had produced effects that were more nobly distinct and lasting.

In the tracks of Cutler came another brigade of college boys from Yale, the "Illinois Band," still another in the "Yale-Dakota Band"; and more from Andover in the "Iowa Band," who built Grinnell College. Then came Marcus Whitman, who went through to Washington and Oregon and back, on a ride as memorable as Paul Revere's, through blizzards and Sioux on the warpath, carrying New Testaments and the destiny of the West in his saddle-bags. He is buried out there on the trail. Indeed, every mile to Oregon is marked by a home-missionary's tombstone.

They all took to heart Cutler's admonition about building schools; they left a string of schools and colleges from Boston to California. We would expect that of the Congregationalists: their missionary zeal has run the course of their history side by side with a passion for education. Harvard they built, in the very year that Roger Williams left them; they built Yale and Williams, Dartmouth, Bowdoin, Amherst, Middlebury, Oberlin and thirty-two more for their men; they founded Mount Holyoke, Smith, Wellesley, Wheaton, for their girls. More than one hundred institutions of higher learning came from their Church; Congregational ministers founded the educational systems of Ohio, Michigan and Oregon and a Congregational minister secured the passage of the ordinance which reserved every sixteenth section of land in several western states for maintaining free education.

Southward, too, they hunted their frontiers. A Colonel Armstrong (he helped stop Pickett at Gettysburg and he commanded a Negro regiment) went down to Hampton, Virginia, to save the Negro from himself after the war had saved him from slavery. "There are more battles to be fought, and I must fight them," said the Colonel. When his friends approached him with the statement that it was impossible for him to do very much for the black man, Armstrong answered, "What are Christians put into the world for but to do the impossible in the strength of God?" He found Hampton a squalid little village with five thousand free, crowded, cowed, squalid, poor and idle Negroes; he left behind him, at death, a Hampton Normal and Industrial Institute which did more for the Negro than a hundred civil wars could ever have done. A boy named Booker T. Washington graduated from his school.

Browne, Bradford, Hooker, Edwards, Cutler, Armstrong—six noblemen of God. And there are more on the Congregationalist roll: Finney, the evangelist who was president of Oberlin, and Moody, who left a shoestore to shake America with his preaching, with singing Sankey at his side; educators Mark Hopkins (someone said, "My idea of a college is a log with Mark Hopkins on one end and a student on the other"), president of Williams, and Timothy Dwight, head of Yale, who converted one-third of the student body of Old Eli and started a series of campus revivals all over the country, and Horace Bushnell, who most successfully restated the truths of religion in terms of human life and experience; Cyrus Hamlin, who could bake bread for an army and build a Roberts College; Henry Ward Beecher (trolley-car conductors passing his Plymouth Church in Brooklyn called out "Beecher Station!") and his sister, Harriet, who wrote *Uncle Tom's Cabin*. And where do we carve the name of Francis E. Clark—"Father Endeavor" Clark—who fathered an interracial, interdenominational, international crowd of youngsters in eighty thousand C. E. Societies spread across eighty-seven countries, who raise their right hands in their conventions, à la Hitler, and shout, "I will be Christian"?

They were great men, sent to meet great crises in American life. They were men-of-the-forward-look, of the frontier-hunting brand, never so much on their knees to their Puritan fathers as on their toes for their children's children. They have always been ready to adapt themselves. When the Great Awakening came, they met it with a new theology; when the Social Awakening came and the demand for a social gospel, they were ready with Washington Gladden and Josiah Strong, who pleaded eloquently for social and economic justice and a Christian social order. When youth was needed to replace age in the pews, Clark was there; and when, in 1913, the whole American Church was faced with the crying need of a new and more relevant statement of faith, the Congregationalists met at Kansas City and created a document which deserves a place at the side of the Declaration of Independence in the Library of Congress. Said they there:

> "We believe in God the Father, infinite in wisdom, goodness and love; and in Jesus Christ His Son . . . and in the Holy Spirit. . . . We are united in striving to know the will of God as taught in the Holy Scriptures, and in our purpose to walk in the ways of the Lord. . . . We believe in the freedom and responsibility of the individual soul, and the right of private judgment. We hold to the autonomy of the local church and its independence of all ecclesiastical control. We cherish the fellowship of the churches . . ."

They have indeed cherished the fellowship of the churches! In 1924 they united with the Evangelical Protestant Church of North America and in 1931, the Christian Church, one hundred thousand strong, joined forces with them. So today, their name appears in the census of the churches as "The Congregational and Christian Churches." All one body, we!

Thus have they been true to their heritage. Apostles of liberty, preachers of freedom, advocates of peace and good will, missionaries and enthusiasts for religious education, they have swayed and steadied us from Plymouth to today. We have adopted the dress of the Puritan and cast off the lace of the Cavalier; we wear our hair cut short in the style which gave the name "Roundhead" to the Puritan, as against the flowing wig of the Court of King Charles; we have adopted his ideals of government, we have copied and borrowed and learned more from the Puritan than we sometimes admit. It might be well for us now to copy more of his staunch virtue and moral grandeur and his steadfast devotion to God. There is nothing we need more.

THE REFORMED CHURCH IN AMERICA

CHAPTER III

THE REFORMED CHURCH IN AMERICA

IN THE chill dawn-fog of a September morning, in
the year of Our Lord 1609, the keel of a Dutch ship
slid to anchor in the waters of New York Bay. It was
the first appearance of the flag of Holland on this side
of the Atlantic; it was the *Half Moon,* out of Amsterdam, and the object of her search was not New York but
a northwest passage to India. Eighteen brave sailors
aboard her answered "Aye, aye, Sir," to Captain Henry
Hudson, who was to get three hundred and twenty dollars for his trip, and eighty dollars more for his wife if he
failed to come back. He came back—without finding
the mythical passage. Sailing up the river which he
found spilling into the bay, he turned back at Albany,
where he found the end of salt water; no salt meant no
ocean beyond; no ocean beyond meant no way out to
Calcutta and Bombay. He went home and reported.
The Dutch East India Company put his report in a
pigeonhole and forgot it. Hudson had failed them. He
had found nothing.

These Dutch were born sailors, never so much at home
as when before the mast; the hulls of their merchant

ships were soaked in the brine of the seven seas. Flying Dutchmen were everywhere, skimming the deep in search of markets and trade. It was a habit with them, a habit formed during the Crusades, when they gazed long and hard on the riches of the East and resolved to have their share. They were great merchants, great traders. But never great colonizers. They loved the homeland too much for that.

They loved their Holland (or, more properly, their Netherlands) so much that they bathed every inch of it with their rich red blood. We think of Holland as the home of quaint windmills and red poppies and wooden shoes. It is so much more than that. Holland has been the scene of the noblest struggle for freedom ever staged upon this earth; historically, it has been the cockpit of revolution. While Jesus was a boy toddling about the streets of old Nazareth, the Dutch were struggling against the very Romans who crucified Him and giving them the fight of their lives. Outnumbered and crushed, they defied their conquerors from the dust, shouting, "We will be free!" When royal inter-marriage bound them and their destinies to the French House of Burgundy, they not only defended themselves against the foreigner but forced from him the famous "Groot Priviligie," a charter of liberties which gave them a representative legislative body with the right to levy taxes, regulate business, coin money and declare war;

when more intermarriage joined them to the Catholic rulers of Catholic Spain, they moaned their old cry from the racks and dungeons of the Spanish Inquisition: "We will be free." Bloody Duke of Alva hanged or beheaded eighteen thousand of them and left one hundred thousand abandoned homes in his crimson wake, but he could not bind them in the iron fold of Rome. Under gallant William the Silent, Prince of Orange, they reached the zenith of their glory; they rose in a welter of blood to drive the invader forever from their shores. They were whipped and they should have known it, a thousand times. But that's a peculiarity of the Dutchman: he never knows when to surrender.

Great sailors, great soldiers, great Protestants. "We will be free" was as much a religious battlecry as a political. They resented foreign domination, in whatever cloak. So when Martin Luther sounded the tocsin of revolt against the Pope, in 1517, they were immediately his enthusiastic allies. They formed the *Reformed* branch of Protestantism; they followed, for the most part, the lead of the three great contemporaries of Luther: Calvin, Melanchthon and Zwingli. (Calvin, the lynx-eyed administrator of Geneva, gave them their Presbyterian form of government and their doctrine; Melanchthon, the timid retiring scholar of the Reformation, gave them their love of scholarship and culture; Zwingli was their fighting soul, their real father, their gay young rebel leader who died in pitched battle with the Catholics.) The main difference between the two churches lay in their interpretation of the meaning of the sacrament of the Lord's Supper; the Lutherans held that the actual body and blood of Christ was "in, with and under" the bread and wine, while the Reformed churchmen held that the bread and wine were only symbols and the whole sacrament a "memorial." That might not bring about a split in the church of our day; to the sixteenth-century fathers it was a serious matter, on which salvation depended.

By the end of the sixteenth century, roving Dutch sea traders ruled the waves, while in culture, education and the art of government, their countrymen at home were two centuries ahead of the rest of Europe. Already there was a system of *public* education, a government of, by and for the people, a written constitution which bears marked resemblance to a constitution drawn up in Philadelphia in 1787, and a group of petty states welded together in a union, or a United States of Holland. Historians who know insist that we have scarcely a legal or political institution of English origin; they give most credit to the Dutch.

In that century, too, Holland had become a haven of refuge for the persecuted Protestants of all Europe. Behind the dikes rested the Pilgrim Fathers, Huguenots from France, Palatines from Germany and Covenanters from Scotland: the very peoples who were, a few years hence, to drive the Dutch from their foothold in America. But that would have meant nothing to the Netherlanders, had they known it. For religious tolerance was as much a national virtue with them as their love of political independence. Their States-General declared that "all religions ought to be tolerated," and granted freedom of conscience to all. Which was something of a virtue in the sixteenth century and something of an improvement on even Puritan character.

With the *Half Moon* tied up in Amsterdam, other Dutch ships pulled their anchors and made for the "River from the Mountains," which Hudson had discovered, to see what they could find. They found enough to make them rock the highlands of the Hudson with their cheers. They found fur and fur meant gold. Little trading-posts began to dot both banks of the river from "Manhattas Harbor" to its upper limit, and dour Dutchmen with their long pipes and pantaloons were soon driving hard bargains with the Indians; in 1623 the Dutch West India Company sent out thirty families of Dutch and Walloon Protestants to settle Fort Nassau (Camden) and Fort Orange (Albany). The English protested; everything from Plymouth to Virginia was theirs, they said. The Dutch listened, puffed at their pipes and sent more colonists. In 1626, Peter Minuit, Reformed Church elder, came over as director-general of the movement. Peter was a trader, too; he traded a bagful of blankets, copper kettles, Jamaica rum and beads (worth twenty-four dollars), for the whole of Manhattan Island. On the southern tip of the island he built a fort; he called it New Amsterdam.

There was no minister, no church, in the New Amsterdam of 1626. The Dutchmen had come not to pray, but to trap; for fur and not for faith. But that could not go on; fur or no fur, men will pray, in counting-house or wilderness. So ere long there came two to help the colony pray; two lay ministers, two "Comforters of the Sick," who visited and exhorted and held informal (Reformed) services in the loft above the village horse-mill. Above the loft was a tower; in the tower swung a bell captured from the Spaniards in Porto Rico.

The Dutch did not come out to settle under Minuit as the West India Company had hoped and soon radical measures were being used to make them come. One of these was the "patroon" system. Any member of the company able to plant a colony of fifty people in New Netherlands within four years was offered sixteen miles of river-front property on the Hudson, a monopoly of fishing, grinding, weaving, fowling and fur, the power to make laws and enforce them, the right to hire and fire all schoolmasters and preachers, the privilege of privateering on all enemy ships, and the high-sounding title of Patroon. His colonists were tenant farmers, bound to the land, and there were as many Negro slaves as he wished; the system soon put the Hudson River country under the Dutch flag. All up and down its shores the old Dutch feudalism was being reborn and great Dutch names were being woven into American history (Van Rensselaer, Van Cortlandt). Schools and Reformed Churches were planted; ministers and educators were introduced to the wilderness towns. Dominie Megapolensis preached to the Dutch and to the Indians and built a church at Albany. But it all ended badly, as such experiments always end. Subsidized ministers are never happy; tyrannized school-teachers are forever miserable; tenant farmers are forever dissatisfied. That's what happened along the Hudson: when the colonists came to understand that the system was designed solely for the advantage of the company, they went elsewhere. That was fortunate for the Reformed Church, for it meant that it was to migrate and wax strong on Long Island, in Brooklyn and New Jersey.

The first Reformed clergyman to arrive in America, however, was not Megapolensis; he was Dominie Jonas Michaelius, and he came to Minuit's New Amsterdam in 1628. He founded a church in his first year; it was the first Protestant Church in America, say the Reformed. Minuit and the village storekeeper were his elders and they helped him serve the first Lord's Supper, to fifty happy Dutchmen and their "guede vrows." He was a versatile soul, this Dominie, and an accommodating one; he went out of his way to serve the Supper to the French-speaking Walloons in the colony. He read the ritual in French. Read it, because he could not speak it.

Michaelius was followed by Dominie Bogardus, who came over in the same ship with the second Governor, Wouter Van Twiller. Washington Irving called the Governor "Wouter, the Doubter" (for he could never make up his mind) and said he looked like a beer barrel on skids. He smoked eight hours, doubted eight hours and slept the other eight. Rarely did he rouse himself to make a decision; he let nature take its course and the colony develop as it would. He and his people grew fat, generous and benevolent together; substantial houses of Dutch brick and tile lined the muddy thoroughfares, with Dutch weathervanes on the roof trees to tell which way the wind was blowing. Only when a storm approached did they rouse themselves to watch the vanes; sometimes, not even then.

After Van Twiller came William (The Testy) Kieft, and with him trouble and turbulence. Brisk, wiry and waspish, he had "two little gray eyes, his nose turned up and the corners of his mouth turned down, pretty much like the muzzle of an irritable pug dog." Kieft was a rascal and Dominie Bogardus (bless his memory!) fought him from start to finish. Corruption gnawed at the vitals of his government from within and wars with the

Indians bothered him without. He built a great wall against Indian attack, across the lower end of the island. We have a street in its place, called Wall Street. He did one good turn for Dominie Bogardus, however, before he died. He helped build a meetinghouse. It seems there was a wedding—a wedding with wine. After the fifth round of drinking, the Dominie let them "subcribe what they were willing to give toward the church. All then with light heads subscribed largely, competing with one another, and although some well repented it when they recovered their senses, they were nevertheless compelled to pay." And lo, the name of William Kieft led all the rest! He paid, too. Today there are ten churches in New York City worshiping under the name of the Collegiate Dutch Reformed Church of New York, which are the direct descendants of the Church in the Fort, built by Bogardus, under Kieft.

William the Testy passed and a wooden-legged one came to replace him. Wooden-legged, oaken-hearted, gruff and grumpy in a kindly sort of way, Peter Stuyvesant was to rule the Dutch colony in its last days. He declared he would rule them as a father rules his children; he proved a hard parent to get along with. He made stringent laws against drinking and saw them fail; he forced the Indians to buy trading licenses—from himself! He extended his despotism to the Church; hating all Lutherans, Independents and Baptists as he hated the devil, he proclaimed that there should be no public religious meetings save those of the Dutch Reformed Church. He banished Browne, the Quaker, from Long Island; he flogged another in Manhattan; he would have gone farther had not the Company stopped him. It was a sad exception to the Dutch rule of tolerance.

Peter had a sword that rattled, that was thirsty for conquest. He drew it against the Swedes in Delaware and won; he drew it against the English and lost. On a hot August day in 1664, he looked out over the bay to see the guns of two British men-o'-war pointed, broadside, at New Amsterdam. Peter stormed and swore he would die rather than surrender. He primed his guns and made ready to fight, but wiser, cooler heads prevailed upon him to prevent a needless slaughter. The Dutch were outnumbered, surrounded. The two Dominies Megapolensis talked him out of his foolhardy wrath, and he surrendered. The Dutch flag came down and, with the British colors commanding the land from Florida to Maine, the dream of a Dutch empire in America was done.

The Dutch played their parts well after the surrender; they were Christian to a superlative degree. For thirty years after the capitulation the English were given free use of the Church in the Fort; every Sabbath, after the Hollanders had ended their morning worship, the service of the Church of England was read to the garrison.

That must have been hard.   Imagine it: a Dutch Church
in an English colony, with Holland and Britain at war
across the sea!   Some found it too hard, gave up the
struggle and returned to Holland.   When the Dutch
ministers found it necessary to raise their own salaries
by begging from door to door, many of them rebelled.
It was degrading, disgusting; Dominie Samuel Megapolensis sailed for Amsterdam; so did Dominie Blom of
Kingston.   Dominie Schaats of Albany wanted to go,
but he was too poor to buy a ticket.   By 1670, there
were just two able-bodied ministers left to care for the
whole Reformed Church in America.   Two men against
a continent!   No church ever rallied to win more
gloriously.   Undermanned, poverty-stricken, ruled by
the hated English, the Dutch Church honored the
heritage of their fathers by failing to know when they
were beaten, by never dreaming of surrender.   They
pooled their resources, reopened their churches, began
again to bring over ministers from Holland, and the day
was saved.

Hardly had New Amsterdam become New York when
the English determined that the Reformed Church must
go and that the Church of England should dominate the
scene.   Secret orders came from England; a campaign
of secret proselyting and open force began.   The British
had promised "liberty of conscience in divine worship
and discipline"; they never meant a word of it.   It

would have been better for them if they had, for their short-sighted campaign of petty tyranny only spurred the Dutch on; they fought it out until, in 1696, they were granted the first ecclesiastical charter in the history of the colony and the only one ever granted, except to the Church of England; the charter gave them a name: *The Protestant Dutch Church of the City of New Yorke.* Now they were a body "Politik," a church in their own right.

In 1720, Frelinghuysen came. Theodore J. Frelinghuysen, German pietist and clerical cyclone, sent to preach piety to the Dutch of New Jersey. He preached a piety that struck a fire wherever it hit. He preached conversion and he preached revival. And he preached with heat. He stormed against the dead formalism and the deadly orthodoxy of the Colonial Church; he found the churches full of stale air and dust and drowsy Dutchmen; he filled the air with holy lightning, stirred the dust mightily and brought the sleepers up straight in their pews. Congregations applauded or rebelled; Frelinghuysen didn't care which, so long as they showed life enough to do either. His brother preachers disagreed over his message and drew off into two rival camps, into the quick and the dead. That didn't bother him either; they were already, unofficially, divided like that. He led his Church into the Great Awakening and gave it a position of leadership which it had to the end, while other, larger churches lagged behind. If you would feel the pulse of the Awakening, put your finger on the Dutch Reformed Church; if you would know the Dutch Reformed Church, then study Frelinghuysen. He is the leader of the age, the tall one of his flock, the essence of their truth.

Meanwhile, there had been trouble brewing with the mother Church in Amsterdam. Under the existing order, candidates for the ministry in America were forced to travel to Holland for ordination. The Classis of Holland (the ruling body) might or might not ordain them when they got there; it was all very uncertain and very unsatisfactory. Sometimes the ministers in America threw discretion to the winds and ordained them themselves, in defiance of Amsterdam; more often they asked permission to do so and waited weeks, months, for a reply, with the candidate cooling his heels at the door of the church. The years dragged on with young men, by the score, turning away from the Church. Jealousies arose; spies trotted back and forth across the Atlantic; a bad split came in the ranks of the Reformed Church clergy, to be breached finally by the efforts of saintly John Livingston, who pushed through a plan of union which not only reunited the clergy but set them free forever from foreign control.

Now, surely, after these long struggles, they could rest. They had earned it. But they did not get it, for the echoes of the battle with Amsterdam were still in the air when the storm of the Revolution broke over the land. When that test came, there was no doubt as to where the men of the Reformed Church would throw their weight: they had no love for England. A bell in the belfry of the old Middle Church became New York's Liberty Bell and the sons of the grizzled campaigners against Alva stepped lightly out of the pew into the ranks of the Continental Army. New Jersey and New York were the seat of Reformed strength in America; New Jersey and New York were also the testing-ground of the Revolution. Here bluff General Herkimer, Dutchman, stopped St. Ledger; leaning against a tree, with a leg shattered by a Hessian ball, he directed the battle and won it; a few days later he died of his wound, propped up in bed puffing his Dutch pipe and reading the Thirty-eighth Psalm. (Every Dutch home in the Mohawk Valley mourned a loss after Herkimer's victory.) Out of the Dutch Church, too, came other heroes, General Schuyler, Colonels Gansevoort, Van Cortlandt and DuBoys; Dominie Romeyn of Hackensack lost everything he owned, Dominie Foering was thrown from his house on a winter midnight and died of exposure. Dominie Hardenbergh was hunted from pillar to post and slept constantly with his hand on a loaded gun. Their churches were defiled, destroyed; they became prisons, stables, cavalry schools, hospitals, smoking ruins. The Dutch were badly beaten, but—they never surrendered.

Free at last as Cornwallis gave up, they set themselves to the task of organizing their free Church and, with their old principles of equality and democracy uppermost in their minds, they created a superb ecclesiastical organization. It was a Presbyterian form of government and it is still in operation. Local churches were placed in charge of ministers (preaching elders) and a *consistory* (composed of lay, *ruling* elders) ; churches were grouped into a Classis and above the Classis was the Particular Synod. At the top of the pyramid was the supreme body of the Church, the General Synod. By 1791, General Synod had established the doctrine of the Reformed Church, basing it on the Belgic Confession, the Heidelberg Catechism and the Canons of the early Synod of Dort. Except for a few minor changes, this is still the polity and doctrine of the Reformed Church in America. When the Constitution of the Church was adopted, in 1792, there was a confusion of names: the denomination was known both as the Dutch Reformed Church in North America and the Reformed Dutch Church in the United States of America; in 1819 the Church was incorporated as the Reformed Protestant Dutch Church. That was too awkward; in 1867 came the name they use today: the Reformed Church in America.

New Year's Day of 1800 found the Reformed Church done with the worst of its struggling and massing her forces for the two great efforts which have occupied them to the present hour: the fight for schools and the missionary enterprise. Education had always been their forte, their hobby; learning and piety were never once divorced in the Dutch mind. When William the Silent sailed to the relief of old Leyden, he offered the gallant defenders one of two prizes: relief from taxation, or a university. They chose the university; from it came most of the early Reformed preachers in America. When Benjamin Franklin began to wonder about electricity, he played with lightning in the tower of old Middle Dutch Church. When the Church in the Fort was built, a School in the Fort was built beside it. No wonder the historians of the Revolution speak of the "powerful Dutch Church" of Revolutionary America; they had in mind not the numerical strength of the communion, but the fact that the leaders, from Dominie Michaelius down, had been university-trained. These ministers, naturally, were vitally concerned with the education of their youth. They built grade-schools, academies, at first, and then colleges. The records of the Collegiate School of New York City date from 1637; of later date but equal influence were the schools on Long Island, in New Jersey and the Mohawk Valley and the Middle West.

Then death gave birth to Rutgers College. Two brothers of Dominie Frelinghuysen died on shipboard while returning from their studies in Holland; that sent the elder brother, Theodore, riding up the Hudson, preaching the gospel of higher education, pleading for an American college for American ministers. Death claimed him before he could realize his dream, but his sons saw it come: in 1776 New Jersey's Governor Franklin (son of Benjamin) granted a charter to "Queen's College." Later, it was rechristened Rutgers. Would that Dominie Frelinghuysen could come riding out of Glory to behold those great men of America who have passed through the portals of his school! Presidents of colleges and of railroads; senators and Supreme Court justices and a vice-president of the United States, lawyers, doctors, merchants, ministers.

On a hilltop above the Rutgers campus was planted the first theological seminary in the United States. That was logical, for to the Dutch theology was the queen of the sciences. So they built the Theological Seminary of the Reformed Church in America, at New Brunswick. Later, in the West, came Hope College, in Michigan, with another Seminary (Western) at her doors, to care for the sons of those hardy Reformed pioneers who had planted their Church in the West.

Union College, Schenectady, was theirs too; it was the first college to be chartered west of the Hudson

River. Into the charter were written these words: "This institution shall never exclude any person of any religious denomination from equal liberty and the advantage of education. . . ." And on its seal is written: "In essentials, unity; in non-essentials, liberty; in all things, charity." That says more than volumes could say for the spirit which lies at the heart of the Reformed Church.

Union and Rutgers are theirs no longer, but they still hold two great colleges of A-1 rank: Hope in Michigan and Central in Iowa.

Ardent as they were in education, they were even more determined in their nineteenth-century missionary crusade. The work this Church has done in winning the world to Christ has been far, far in advance of what might be expected of so small a body of believers. They have been hunting the frontier posts of the missionary line since the days of Admiral Coligny the Huguenot, since 1557, which means that they had the first foreign missionary in the field. In 1624 there were two "Comforters of the Sick" in Formosa; shortly after, they were appearing in India with their Bibles and their catechisms. It was the missionary impulse which sent the first ministers to New Netherlands; those preachers came not only to preach to the Dutchmen but to plead for the soul of the Indian. Dominie Megapolensis had been converting Indians for four years before John Eliot converted his first in New England.   Not a bad start for a small church.

The General Synod of 1817 vowed it would "spread the Gospel among the Indians of North America, the Inhabitants of Mexico and South America and in other portions of the heathen and anti-Christian world." They have done that and more. They have thrown a cordon of Reformed missionaries around the globe. A queer kind of missionary.   A missionary quite anxious to preach Christ as he knew Him, in his own Church, but always ready to co-operate with the evangelists of other denominations when the situation demanded it!   They did not strive to make the world a "Reformed" world, to mold all men to their ecclesiastical pattern; they wanted the world for Christ. Conscious of their limited constituency, they once merged their forces one hundred per cent with the American Board of Commissioners for Foreign Missions. They labor today under their own Board, for that seems to them, after experiment, to be the best way to do their job. But when the final history of American missions is written, one uncontested honor will be theirs: they have led the way in placing Christ before sect.

Their missionary heroes are legion; a hundred volumes might not tell enough of their deeds, a thousand sing their praises honestly. Their greatest were Scudder of India and Verbeck of Japan. Scudder was a doctor who fought disease with the point of his Christian lancet; few medical men have done such healing, anywhere in God's world. He and his family, it is intimated, have given one thousand years of service to foreign missions! And Verbeck? Guido Verbeck is more responsible for the government of modern Japan than any Japanese. He gave them not only that, but a great university and their whole modern educational system as well, and when the first deputation of Japanese came touring the West, humble little missionary Verbeck came with them, with their highest decoration, the Order of the Rising Sun, on his breast. He is without peer in his influence on the development of a new civilization in the Sunrise Kingdom.

Leaders of organized religion fall often into common error; they think of big churches as churches with many members, with great cathedrals, colleges, programs. The Reformed Church in America has made that sort of measurement ridiculous. It has come out of the biggest little country in the world and made itself the biggest little church in Christendom. It has given to America gifts without compare: Santa Claus at Christmas, and a deep trust in the manger's Babe; colored eggs at Easter and a sense of the risen Christ. From it came the first gestures toward a union of the States, toward voting by ballot and representative government, toward our written Constitution and our Declaration of Independence.

It has inspired us with the dream of a free church in a free state; the will to freedom has leaped from it to us as a spark between two poles. It has encouraged culture and fought ignorance, stood for a trained ministry preaching to an intelligent laity. And with but few glaring exceptions, it has led the churches and the people of the churches in the high art of religious tolerance.

The Reformed have been tolerant, but they have stood stoutly by what they have conceived to be the truth, by their Calvinism. They have seldom surrendered to religious fad or social fancy; nothing merely new and novel has gained credence with them at the expense of their ancient, dogged trust in Christianity as a revealed religion and in the Bible as God's Word. They have produced no great preachers of the social gospel, no lobbyists, no political parsons; barring a few brief sorties in the fight for temperance and Sabbath observance, they have let all that strictly, severely alone. They have spent themselves on the root truths of faith, on Christ and Him Crucified, the Hope of the World; they have insisted quietly, tolerantly, stubbornly that this is the business of their Church, and its message. Nothing matters but that. They will stick to it and it will be well for the rest of us if they do. With a new sect coming with each new dawn, with clever, catchy formulas for social salvation greeting us at every new turn of the road and vanishing, uselessly, at the next, it will be good for us to listen to them as they plead the cause of the undying God at the heart of things, as they lift our eyes to the presence of the risen Christ in our midst and tune our ears to hear Him speak. If they can but do that, they shall yet do greater things than they have already done.

THE LUTHERANS

CHAPTER IV

THE LUTHERANS

EISENACH was a tiny town in 1492, so tiny and un-
important that Christopher Columbus, who was busy
right then discovering America, had in all probability
never heard of it. He probably had never heard of a
lad named Martin Luther, either, who, while Columbus
was pacing the deck of the *Santa Maria,* was playing a
lute and singing for coins in Eisenach's quaint and quiet
streets. No one paid much attention to Martin Luther
in those days, for no one knew that this stolid, sturdy,
black-eyed German boy would one day outdo, outdis-
cover Columbus. The great Genoese only found a new
world; the German gave men a new heaven. Greatness,
great men, great deeds, move among us like the angels,
while we are unaware.

Eisenach's lutist became, in time, the prince of this
world's liberators, the creator of the modern man, the
fighting father of Protestantism. We know too well
what he did to repeat it here; we know how he broke the
strangle hold of a rotten Rome on the throat of the
Western world; how he tore off the chains that locked
the Scriptures away from the eyes of common folk, how

he translated the Book from Latin into the common tongue; how he ripped off the lid of a late and improved Pandora's box to set in motion the great creative forces of education, faith and freedom which have made us what we are.   His place is secure; should every other hero of the race perish tomorrow, there would still be Luther, alone at Worms, defying Rome with one fist and clutching the Book with the other, saying to the ages, "Here I stand.   God help me.   Amen."

He gave us a new Church, a new Book, a new world; he left men standing with their ancient shackles, broken, in their hands.   His Smaller Catechism became the spiritual Baedeker of the strongest Protestant Church in the world and the basic tenets of his faith have influenced all the rest of Protestantism.   His boyish lute lies broken on the grave of time, its tunes long since forgotten; his manly works and giant faith live on, an anthem and a cry of hope for those who are yet to be.

Now Luther based his battle and his hopes on three great principles.   Said he, "The just shall live by faith!" That was Alpha and Omega, the beginning and the end. Not by penance pennies, nor by altar prayers.   By faith! Again, he said that the individual conscience was responsible to God alone.   Conscience, not the Pope, was King; God, not the priests nor cardinals, was the ultimate authority.   And yet again, he held that the Bible was the clear, perfect, inspired and authoritative Word of God and guide of man.   God, conscience and the Book.   He left these for his followers to build upon.

They builded well.   Meeting at Augsburg in 1530, they worked out, with his help, their "Augsburg Confession," which they have held forever since to be the true expression of the fundamental doctrines of Holy Writ; it was their fundamental symbol, their second cornerstone.   And it is the head of the corner of Protestantism.   Lutherans everywhere hold to that Confession in its *unaltered* form; on it and on Luther's trinity of God-conscience-and-the-Book, they have built their house.   There is no sand beneath that house, nor has there ever been.   When Luther sang

"A mighty fortress is our God,
    A bulwark never failing . . ."

he might almost have been singing of the Church he left behind him.   For that is just what it has come to be. The winds have blown upon it, to no avail.   A thousand isms, from Rationalism to Humanism, have tried to storm its walls and perished in the storming; mankind has marched and struggled and fallen and risen to march again and always, above the smoke of its fighting, the Lutheran Church has held her place on those old foundations, solid, immovable, on a rock.

Of course, such a movement, such a gift as this could not be confined to Augsburg, or Wittenberg, or Germany, or Europe. It took wings, crossed national boundaries faster than the birds could fly, becoming rooted in France, England, Norway, Denmark, Finland, Sweden, Iceland, Greenland, America. Lutheran tars reefed sail and spread it before the masts of the early explorers; Lutherans followed the trails of the South American Conquistadores a century before the Pilgrims touched Plymouth Rock; Lutherans fought the Indian with Roundhead and Cavalier, settled with the earliest Quaker and Patroon. In 1619, sixty-five Lutheran sailors pushed through to build a cluster of huts on the west shore of Hudson's Bay, where their ships froze in for the winter. Scurvy got at them, and the bitter cold; when they cut their way out in the spring and headed for the open sea and home, there were just three of them left. But the date of their coming is a peg to hang things on: from 1619 on, there were Lutheran services in America.

There were services in New Netherland and Albany, with the Dutch looking on. Furtive services they were, for the Dutch were resolved to keep their colonies safe for the Dutch and the Dutch Reformed. The Lutherans imported a pastor from Amsterdam, one John Ernst Goetwasser, about the time that Jonas Bronck (Lutheran) was becoming noted as a peacemaker with the Indians. (The *Bronx* is named for him.) Peter Stuyvesant ordered the dominie out and the Lutherans hid him in a barn for two years before peevish Peter had his way and Goetwasser left his haymow for Amsterdam. Abelius Zetskoorn, a student, came next to preach and fared little better. Stuyvesant hustled him down the Delaware. But the stubborn Lutherans fought until the English came, when things were easier. Meanwhile they had spread out over Albany, New Jersey, Long Island and the Delaware.

The Delaware! It was alive, just then, with Swedes. And all good Swedes were good Lutherans. The first of them came out under a "Commercial Company" organized at the royal command of the great King Gustavus Adolphus, the fighting Lion of the North, who fought and conquered Europe from the Rhine to the Oder, from the Baltic to the Alps. To finance the marches of his Swedes and to Christianize the Indian, he planned to settle a New Sweden in America, near the Dutchman's New Netherland, where fur and golden treasure were to be had for the taking. Poor King Gustavus! He was killed at the battle of Luetzen before he could work out his dream. His daughter, Queen Christina, sat his throne for a while, then deserted her homeland for Paris.

The Swedes liked Christina, at that. They named their first American settlement after her; it was Fort Christina, on the Delaware. Thence came the first preachers to preach: good Reorus Torkillus and saintly John Campanius and some others who were less worthy of their robes. Churches were built wherever they were needed. Two of them are with us yet: Gloria Dei, in Philadelphia and Old Swede's in Wilmington.

On the boat with Campanius arrived John Printz, Governor John Printz, Pennsylvania's first governor, who built Pennsylvania's first capital on Tinicum Island and who weighed four hundred pounds. And who, like Christina, just got tired of his job and quit it. That was a bit of luck for John Printz; ere long Peter Stuyvesant marched on New Sweden in a higgledy-piggledy war, took Fort Christina, pulled down the flag of the Swedes. It stayed down.

A full century after the collapse of the Swedes on the Delaware, another Lutheran caravan slipped into the South, into Georgia, led by a British General who felt sorry for them. Oglethorpe, searching Europe for colonists, heard the story of the Salzburgers of Austria, who for two hundred years had maintained their Protestant Lutheran faith in the face of Catholic persecution and of their march, when they were torn from their children and exiled, from Austria to Germany and England. He brought fifty families of them to Georgia, where they built a town and a church twenty-five miles north of Savannah and called both Ebenezer. Two preachers were with them, teaching them to hate slavery and love the Indian. They built mills, schools and the first orphanage in America, and they gave to Georgia her first governor: John Adam Treutlen. Then the furies that had lost them on the road from Austria caught up with them again; one of their own pastors betrayed them to the British in the Revolutionary War and the British burned Ebenezer to the ground and scattered the luckless inhabitants across the Carolinas. There their descendants live today.

German Lutherans trickled down from the Palatine into Pennsylvania, building a string of settlements long before Penn, from Printz's Tinicum Island to the Indian outposts in the wilderness. The Indians liked them, admired their industry and their honesty, got along with them better than they got along with Puritan or Cavalier. They liked one Lutheran especially, going so far as to adopt him into their (Mohawk-Iroquois) tribe. He was Conrad Weiser: from the day of his adoption to the day of his death he signed every treaty with the Indians in the Pennsylvania territory. We can thank him for this: he cast the deciding vote in the Iroquois powwow that decided that the Iroquois should fight with the English and not with the French. When the Revolution came, his influence swung the tribe away from the English and with the Americans. Which meant that this nation was to be English instead of French, then American instead of English, with an Anglo-Saxon culture instead of a Latin, with a Protestant faith instead of a Roman Catholic.

Conrad Weiser had not yet joined his fathers when his daughter married the greatest Lutheran ever to live and move and have his being in America. Some call him Germany's greatest gift to America; all know him as Henry Melchior Muhlenberg. He is the patriarch of American Lutheranism, called as surely to lead them as Washington was called, a little later, to lead his nation. He came at a desperate hour, when the country was rocking under the impact of a great German immigration (seven thousand entered Philadelphia alone in 1749) and when the Lutheran Church was finding itself quite unable to care for them. They were fast becoming the victims of traveling spiritual charlatans and vagabonds. Efficient ministers were few and far between; what Lutheran Churches there were, were isolated, provincial in their outlook, suspicious of one another. Muhlenberg burst upon them with a motto: "Ecclesia Plantanda." (The Church must be planted.) He laid them all upon the anvil of his own passionate consecration to that ideal, shamed them out of their exclusive selfishness, bound them together with the fiery bond of his spirit as the old Roman father had once bound together his bundle of sticks. He gave them a uniform liturgy and a glorious one; he organized the first synod (the Lutheran ruling body, composed of laymen and clergymen) in America and he laid the foundations for a native ministry. He lifted his people out of their colonial, parochial, missionary status and brought into being the independent and self-reliant Lutheran Church in America.

Odd, that this happened just then. Odd, that the birth of the Lutheran Church came but a short generation before the birth of the nation. Odd it will be, from now on, to see how the two came on together, doing almost the same thing at the same time, from one stage of development to the next. But that's just what happened. When the Patriarch died, his sons were off fighting the Revolution. One son, John Gabriel Peter, dramatized the issue for every German Lutheran in America: in the midst of a fiery patriotic sermon, he threw back his clergyman's gown to reveal a soldier's uniform beneath. "There is a time to preach and a time to pray," said Peter Muhlenberg, "but those times have passed away. There is a time to fight! . . ." And this was it. He led his Germans out to fight with Von Steuben and De Kalb and a score more Lutheran commanders. They fought along the whole Continental front, fought Hessians, fought their own flesh and blood. They left their blood on Valley Forge's snows, where one of them managed the gruesome hospital; the Constitution of the Pennsylvania Ministerium was used in the drawing up of the Declaration of Independence and in the formation of the Constitution of the United States; a Lutheran "bellman old and gray" rang the Liberty Bell; Lutheran women, in a Lutheran Church, stitched the first American flag and sent it to snap on the mast of the *Bon Homme Richard;* a Lutheran became the first speaker of the first House of Representatives.

Their war record is a proud one; so is their record in the period of expansion and organization which followed the war, when they followed again, step for step, the expansion and organization of their country. The national frontier leaped the Alleghenies and a flood of native-born and foreigners came up the Mississippi Valley; the Lutheran preachers were hot on their trail, building churches wherever a new settlement appeared, sweeping Germans, Swedes, Norwegians into their membership. By 1825, twenty-five thousand new communicants had been added and there were forty-five thousand Lutherans in the United States. Mushroom towns produced mushroom municipal governments; new synods made their appearance in New York, Ohio and the South. Washington was elected president and Congress was organized; then Adams came and John Quincy Adams and Jefferson. Monroe toured the country and the country cheered; it was "the era of good feeling." There were cheers for Louisiana, just purchased from Napoleon, for the new tariff and the new National Bank. And there was cheering in the Lutheran Church, where an "era of co-operation" was rousing enthusiasm; the Old-World animosities between those of different nationalities were dying out; there began to develop a sympathy, almost a love, for other denominations; there were gestures of union with the Episcopalians and the Dutch Reformed and, as if to parallel the new centralization of power in the Federal Government, the Lutherans created a "General Synod," intended to link them all together in one body, to give them a uniform liturgy and literature, a common confession of faith. There was as much trouble over that General Synod as there was over the new Federal Constitution; some synods were suspicious, afraid of it; some came in and went quickly out again; some never came in at all. It was a noble experiment, a great aspiration, but it never quite worked. At its peak of power in 1860, it never included more than two-thirds of the whole Church.

During this era, too, they met the thrust of Rationalism, at the old foundation of God-conscience-and-the-Book. Spread by French influences and officers during the Revolution, Rationalism brought about a battle in the first days of the peace as fierce as Bunker Hill, as deadly as Valley Forge. Influenced by it, the Pennsylvania Ministerium revised its constitution and struck out all references to the old Lutheran confessions; they asked their preacher-candidates no questions about Augsburg; a New Yorker prepared an English Catechism as a substitute for Luther's and a rationalistic hymnal and liturgy. But it was wasted; the majority of the Church stood stubbornly with their fathers and their fathers' creeds and refused the bait of the radicals.   The old foundations held.   When the storm was over, they found themselves, like a bone that has been broken and mended, even stronger than before.

Through this hectic first half of the nineteenth century, the irresistible forces of an irresistible conflict were mobilizing; an industrial, mechanized North and a feudal, agricultural South, with next to nothing in common, clashed in civil war and the era of Sectionalism was upon us.   So far as the political conflict was concerned, the Lutherans helped elect Lincoln president and multitudes of them joined the Union Army.   One-third of the Federal troops (eight hundred and fifty thousand out of two million seven hundred thousand) were of German birth and direct descent; at least one-half of them were of German ancestry.   And in their Lutheran Church, too, they did a little "sectionalizing" of their own.   That was to be expected, in view of what was happening to the nation.   The tendency toward church union which had marked the era of co-operation had run its course; denominational loyalty had a second birth. Each church began to realize that it had its own peculiar method of doing the King's business; each church had its own private history, customs, creeds.   And each church, from 1830 to 1870 or thereabouts, asserted itself anew and proceeded to go its separate way.   Too bad? Yes, but it happened, just the same.   Methodists, Bap-

tists and Presbyterians were sectionalized, torn asunder
by the Civil War, in company with their smaller brethren; the house of the Lutherans was divided not only
over slavery, but over doctrine as well, and split after
split occurred. The Church, in general, had followed the
flag. Or the flags. The era of discord and explosion was
upon them.

The southern Lutherans were the first to break away;
the Confederates formed their own southern synod soon
after Bull Run. Then during the war and after it, dissension cropped out in General Synod; a minority group
of rebels felt that there should and must be a modifica-
tion of historic Lutheranism; the old standards were all
right, they said, but they should be adapted to the hour;
there should be an "American Lutheranism," stripped
of all those distinctive Old-World traits and practices.
Angry shouts of protest met them; ill-considered epithets
filled the air; congregations divided, friends became enemies, young people dropped away. Then the district
synods got out of hand; New York, Illinois, Buffalo,
Iowa, Pittsburgh seceded from the "union." The old
barrier of language added fuel to the blaze; to preach
in English, or to preach in German (or Swedish, or Norwegian, or Icelandic) . . . aye, that *was* the question.
It was an hour of crisis for the Lutherans, as it was for
those on the battlefields of Dixie.

Both Church and nation came through. "American

Lutheranism" went down to overwhelming defeat at the hands of that vast majority who would not scrap their heritage, who believed that they could live and flourish in the land of their adoption without discarding or adulterating the spiritual treasures of the land of their birth. And when the struggle was over, a General Council stood alongside the old General Synod.

Came Appomattox and the years of reconstruction. The carpetbagger moved into the South and another deluge of emigrants from the north of Europe swung into the Ohio River and Great Lakes country, across the West and Canada. One million seven hundred and fifty thousand Scandinavians came to America between 1870 and 1910; in one year (1882) one hundred thousand sailed up New York Bay; in 1903, seventy-seven thousand. The Lutheran Church, weakened by its years of crisis and struggle, now proceeded to perform the miracle of the age. It threw open its doors to that flood, met it squarely, gathered in its strength. By 1870, there were four hundred thousand Lutherans in the United States; in 1910, they passed the two-and-one-half-million mark. What had been an assembly-hall of epithet in the years of the crisis had become, overnight, a beehive of earnest Christian zeal. It was the day of "big business" for the Lutherans, as it was the day of big mergers, corporations and trusts for Wall Street. The rise of Standard Oil and the great "public service" corporations was duplicated by the development of Lutheran synods, colleges, seminaries, homes for the aged, orphanages, missions; home missionaries followed the wagon trains going West and foreign missionaries hurried out to Africa, India, Japan, doing a "big business" for God. Magnificent cathedrals and pretentious new "church plants" were built everywhere. (We're still paying for some of them!) Big Business, indeed!

Few were aware of it when another phase came: the United States slipped across the line from the days of big business to the day of larger units without benefit of fanfare. Big business helped shove us into the World War in 1917. Lutherans fought that one, too. (Six per cent of the Lutheran congregations went to the war, as compared to four per cent of the general population.) And when the ghastly foolishness of that world conflict was done and we had properly decorated our wounded and buried our dead, we turned, sickened at the thought of it, to ask, "Why?" Why should one nation fight another, in our huddled world? Why all this international misunderstanding? Why did not all the nations come together in one great "Federation of the World"? It became the fashion, all of a sudden, to appreciate our neighbors, to overlook the disruptions of the past, to plot protectively against such disruption on the road that lay ahead. "Get together" was the demand on the tongue of Everyman.

"Get together" soon began to loom up, stronger than ever before, in the mind of the American Church. Why all these Protestant denominations, men wanted to know? Why was Christ's house so divided? Why must there be nineteen different kinds of Methodist, eighteen bodies of Baptist, seventeen brands of Lutheran? "Why don't they all get together?" asked Everyman of Everyman on the street.

The Lutherans set themselves to do just that! As the League of Nations was coming into being at Geneva, a united Lutheran Church was coming into being in America. Here is their second miracle: the Lutherans, with more to overcome than any other Protestant sect or denomination on the globe, with the insurmountable barrier of language and nationality to conquer, with Old-World prejudices and New-World confusions to baffle them, have outstripped all Protestantism in moving toward church union, toward consolidation and conservation of church resources and effort, toward a more respectable and efficient day of larger units in the work of the Kingdom of God. As early as 1820, they had started it. Four synods of Germans joined forces in 1919, to form the Evangelical Lutheran Synod of Wisconsin and Other States. Three synods of Norwegians, in 1917, joined forces to form the Norwegian Lutheran Church of America. During the week of November 11, 1918 (Armistice Week!), forty-five constituent synods in three general bodies (the General Synod, the General Council, the United Synod South) joined to form the United Lutheran Church in America, a merger still without comparison in American church history. In 1930 the Middle West synods of German background formed the American Lutheran Church and later in the same year, the American Lutheran Church, together with two Norwegian synods, a Danish and a Swedish synod, formed the American Lutheran Conference, a federation. The present status of Lutherans in America is that nearly ninety-seven per cent of them are to be found in three main groups: the United Lutheran Church in America, the American Lutheran Conference and the Synodical Conference. So today there are, in fact, not "seventeen different brands of Lutheran," but only three, with a total membership of over four millions of worshipers, presenting a united front and teaching and believing and preaching as a unit, of God and conscience and the Book.

Nor were Lutherans satisfied with mere national organization. The sun never went down on their churches; they were a *world* church and they felt the need of a world-embracing organization to bind it together. They flashed a call across the seas in 1923; twenty-two nations responded, sent delegates to the first Lutheran World Convention (at Eisenach!) to sing *A Mighty Fortress Is Our God*, not as Germans or Norwegians or Canadians

or Americans, but as the common children of a common
Father God.   Our secular League of Nations may have
failed, but the world league of Lutherans is a brilliant
success.   They overcome sectional prejudice and national
bitterness and make boundary lines look foolish; they
give a touch of the absurd to the petty kingdoms of man
in bringing together the workers of a house not made
with hands, the men of the kingdom of God.   They have
strengthened the Church in Soviet Russia, where
churches have become anathema; they have stood gal-
lantly by the gallant Church in Germany, where
Lutherans are fighting with their backs to the wall
against the onslaught of Hitler, to wage the most heroic
fight for God and Christian freedom that our age shall
ever see.   Look down from glory, Martin Luther, and
be comforted!

Such is the story of the Lutherans.   It is a worthy one,
in spite of their many natural mistakes and their quite
human limitations.   Their exclusiveness has hurt them;
their language conflict has obstructed their progress;
their debates over "secret societies" have left blots on
their 'scutcheon.   But why let the blots hide the 'scutcheon, or dwarf the record of their genuine achievement?
From Luther standing alone at Worms in 1521 they have
grown to a world church of eighty-two million souls;
from a German sect of Protestants they have built a

European Lutheran Church embracing sixty million communicants; from a preacher hiding in a barn in Peter Stuyvesant's New Amsterdam they have risen to the status of a church nearly five million strong in the United States, standing third among her sister Protestant denominations. Through their racial groups (Lutheranism is Protestantism's League of Nations) they have poured into our American blood the finest characteristics of the finest racial stocks of northern Europe; as a matter of fact, the dominant characteristics of American character come not so much from New England or the South, as from the racial melting pot of Pennsylvania, New Jersey and New York, where Lutherans have always maintained their finest strength.

They have fought our wars and made lovely our peace; they have rung our Liberty Bells and built thirty-three colleges, thirty-seven seminaries, sixty hospitals, sixty-two orphanages and seventy-seven homes for the aged. But that is all mere scaffolding, mere "outward works" in which any good Lutheran would take small pleasure, mere framework built up around a solid, inner core which will outlast the builders and the building. They build their churches, for instance, in the form of the cross. They can't help that. For if you could slit open the red heart of Lutheranism, you would find buried within it the Cross of Jesus Christ. And if you were to demand of them that they put the meaning of their message and their method and their faith in half a dozen words, they would hold out to you their Holy Bible and say evenly, "Here we stand. God help us."

THE BAPTISTS

CHAPTER V

THE BAPTISTS

(I)

How old are the Baptists? Well, how old are the hills? One date is as hard to determine, to pin down, as another; one beginning is as obscure as the next. That's exceptional. For men and institutions, usually, are quite sure of their birthplaces and dates. The Methodist is sure; there is John Wesley, and Charles. The Lutheran knows; he has his Luther, his Wittenberg. The Presbyterian has Calvin and Geneva. But the Baptists! Say some of them, "We have no founder but Jesus; we were born the day He stood with the Baptist, knee-deep in Jordan. We recognize no human authority, no human creed. Our faith was here, functioning, before the first pope came to Rome; we were Protestant before the Reformation, before Luther was born." Say others, "We began with John Smythe in 1608." What manner of Church *is* this? A company of saints without a patriarch, or with many? A lesser breed without the law?

Hardly that. Let's put it this way. There were many Democrats before Thomas Jefferson, but the Democratic *party* began with him. Just so there were many Baptists before Smythe, but their origin *as a denomination* began with him, in 1608. Driven out on purely historical grounds to prove his case, the "Jordan-birthplace" Baptist is hard put to it to show an unbroken succession of churches from then till now. His churches came irregularly, unconnected one with the other. But he is quite within reason in claiming that his *principles* are as old as Christ in Jordan. And what are those principles?

Baptism! That's first. Baptism of believers. There is no warrant for infant baptism in Scripture, he says. (Nor is there.) Baptism of believers only. Baptism is a public oath of loyalty to Christ, to the Baptist mind, and no babe can take that.

Loyalty to the Scriptures as the final authority! That, to some, is even more important than baptism of believers. No pope, no cardinal, can dictate here; there are no Baptist bishops. Not the Creeds, nor the Confessions. The Scriptures! They hold to that as they hold to Jesus Christ as the lone Lawgiver and King over Church and conscience.

The independence of the local church! What they aim at is not an airtight ecclesiastical organization; what they want is Christian character. Each group of worshipers may ordain, call, dismiss, believe as they will, run their church as they wish. Preacher and laymen have equal power; this is a democracy. If individuality ever had a chance, it has it here.

Complete separation of Church and State! They have never been a State Church, never taken orders from any government or king; in their blood is an eternal insistence that the State shall rule only in affairs political and let the Church alone. They are God's patriots, putting allegiance to Him always above allegiance to Cæsar. Freedom of conscience and complete divorce of Church and State! How they have suffered for that! They have faced mockery and mud, fines, whippings and iron bars; they have been burned at the stake and pulled on the rack, but they have held to it. Their torturers might as well have expected a man to walk without a head as to expect to tear that out of the Baptist. And note this, and remember it: *never once in their bitter, bloody history have they struck back at their persecutors, or persecuted any other for his faith.* That is patriotism touched by the divine.

In one form or another, with one isolated group or another, these ideas persisted through the centuries following Jesus. Heroic groups appeared, here or there, advocating one or all of these basic Baptist principles. But it would be a rash man who would call any of them strictly Baptist groups. He would be a poor scholar who would attempt to trace the Baptists, on available historical evidence, further back, as an organized church, than the twelfth century; he would be a better scholar if he started with the sixteenth. Be it enough to say here that the modern Baptist is the child of the sixteenth-century Anabaptist, the grandchild of the twelfth-century Waldensian.

Nonconformists of first water were the Waldensians; they broke step in the twelfth century with the Roman Catholic Church and were never whipped into line again. They took their name from Peter Waldo of Lyons, who made a fortune and gave it away when he read Christ's advice to the rich young ruler. Coupled with his belief in poverty was his belief that the people should be evangelized in their own language. So he had translators put to work to make the Scriptures readable and took over the evangelizing himself. He won disciples and imposed upon them an iron discipline; he made of them the most obstinate heretics ever chastized by the rods of Rome. Rome drove them out into the caves and valleys of the Alps; they came back when Rome grew tired and went on preaching their way. Today there are fifteen thousand of them.

Waldensian code and doctrine are hard to classify, for they were not a unit in belief. Some retained much Catholic doctrine, with teachers, priests and bishops; others were congregational in polity and highly evangelical, rejecting transubstantiation and all sacramental grace and infant baptism. These evangelists filtered into

Switzerland and Germany, where they deeply influenced the Anabaptists.

Now the Anabaptists ("those who baptize again," or "rebaptizers") were the left wing of the Reformation; they were vagrant seeds in a vagrant wind, wild tares in the field of Rome, shooting up suddenly, unexpectedly, everywhere. Their enemies tried laughing at them, but soon gave it up; the Anabaptist was more dangerous than laughable. Advocating communism, pacifism and the abolition of capital punishment, they rejected infant baptism as contrary to Scripture and asserted the freedom of the soul and the conscience; they demanded the separation of Church and State, refused to take an oath in court, or even to hold civic office, and stood against the payment of taxes and interest on money loaned! That was about as far to the left as any reformer could go; it made them not only heretics to the Church, but rebels to the State. Popes and princes went after them with fire and sword; every great Protestant reformer wrote and spoke against them.

Luther condemned them in Germany when they took the part of the people in the Peasants' War of 1525, advising the princes to "knock down, strangle and stab" them without mercy. That's easy to understand. Luther feared, more than anything else, a war at the heart of his movement of reform; the Anabaptists, on the other hand, in view of their principles, could not help joining in this upheaval for human rights, on the side of the oppressed. Luther, for all his greatness, left the Church still chained to the chariot wheels of the State. The Anabaptist could never stand for that. Hence, he fought with the peasants; hence, he parted with the Lutherans and the Zwinglians and moved on alone, guarding his peculiar heritage, resolved to win with it or die in the attempt.

In Switzerland the Anabaptists were moderate, careful, scholarly. Their leaders were constructive; they translated the Old Testament into German years before Luther thought of it; when persecution drove them from Switzerland, they wrote and preached in Moravia.

The Italian group was short-lived, probably because Rome is in Italy. Driven out, they disappeared in Poland.

The Dutch Anabaptists were ultraradical. Led by Melchior Hoffman, they created a shambles of fanaticism in Münster, committing a series of excesses and outrages which have burdened the whole Anabaptist movement with a mark of shame it never deserved. The result was catastrophic war and bloodshed; a remnant reorganized themselves as Mennonites.

When we reach the Mennonites, we have reached the seventeenth century; and when we reach the seventeenth century, we reach the first of the immediate ancestors of the Baptists. Menno Simons, a priest who deserted the Catholics in 1536 for the Anabaptists, taught that the Scriptures alone were the authority of man's faith and practice; that baptism was a believer's privilege; that church discipline was to be rigorously enforced in business, in the family and in all personal affairs. The limits to which he and his followers went in this matter of discipline were absurd. Be that as it may, the Mennonites were (and still are) a gentle, peaceful, law-abiding, virtuous people. And persistent. The men of Menno knew no discouragement; they plowed through the snows of Russia, they climbed the mountains of Switzerland, they pleaded their cause in the streets of Leipzig and on the dikes of Amsterdam. Somewhere near those dikes they met the English refugee Separatists; somewhere, near there, they met John Smythe and Thomas Helwys and John Morton.

Now Smythe and Helwys and Morton were greeted gladly by the Mennonites in Holland; these men were forged of their own brand of Mennonite steel, blades cut to order for their cause. Smythe had been vicar at Gainsborough; Gainsborough was not far from Scrooby, where Bradford and Brewster lived. He came to Holland in 1606, fleeing James I; by 1609 he had been won over by the Mennonite argument and he was a thoroughgoing Baptist. He rebaptized himself, then Howys, then the rest of them and organized, on the spot, the first English General Baptist Church (general, because they believed in a general atonement, for all men). All went well until Smythe tried to lead his followers over, en masse, into the fold of the Mennonites. That was too much for Helwys and Morton; Baptist or no Baptist, they could never go that far. They were still . . . Englishmen. They excommunicated Smythe, who died in 1612 and who wrote, in the very year of his death, in a Confession for his faithful followers, his conviction that

"The magistrate, by virtue of his office, is not to meddle with religion, or matters of conscience, nor to compel men to this or that form of religion or doctrine, but to leave the Christian religion to the free conscience of every one, and to meddle only with political matters. . . ."

So he went down to the gates of death with his colors flying, staunch Baptist to the end. Helwys and Morton returned to England to "face the music" of persecution for their faith, if need be, and to win, if God please, a few recruits before they died.

They suffered little if at all. The persecutions of James had run their course and only a few, after 1612, paid the drastic penalty. Joan Boucher had been burned for heresy in 1550; Edward Wrightman, the last of the English to die at the stake, was burned in 1611; between the two were scores of others who witnessed with their lives, who paid fines or went to exile or the whipping-post. But the fury had waned by 1612 and the road lay open to the converts of Menno. Probably, Mennonites roamed England before Helwys and Morton came back. If they did, they were not amazingly successful. But they did sow Anabaptist seeds and prepare the soil for later growth.

By 1638, the first *Particular* Baptist Church (Particular, because they believed in a particular or limited atonement, for the elect alone) was organized on English soil; in 1641, another group broke from the General branch, convinced that the only *correct* form of baptism was baptism by immersion. In 1644 these "immersion" Baptists wrote their famous Confession of Faith, which is a guide to millions of Baptists to this day, in which they called themselves "Anabaptists," but *for* which they came to be called, for the first time in history, Baptists.

Through the subsequent periods of storm and quiet in English history the two branches of the Baptists wended their separate ways, contributing lavishly to the enrichment of English life and character. Consistently, they maintained their own freedom; consistently, they kept hammering into the Englishman a love of liberty in all things. For that the English owe a debt to the Baptists they can never pay. They, more than any other, more than Alfred or Henry or the Iron Duke, made England free. And more than Cromwell. Indeed, the Baptists coached Cromwell!   As a prelude to the Revolution, the Confession of 1644 declared that ". . . concerning the worship of God, there is but one lawgiver . . . which is Jesus Christ. . . . So it is the magistrates' duty to tender the liberty of men's consciences (which is the tenderest thing unto all conscientious men . . .) and to protect all under them from all wrong, injury, oppression, and molestation."

Cherishing that and with generations behind them having given their lives for it, it was natural that they should flock into the army of Cromwell as they had flocked in to the Peasants' Revolt.   In the Protector's Irish garrison in 1755, there were twelve Baptist governors of cities, ten colonels, three lieutenant-colonels, ten majors, forty-three company officers.   A daughter of Cromwell married Colonel Fleetwood, a Baptist.   By the thousand, they stood with Cromwell against the King and did as much as any Roundhead to send a shudder across every throne in Europe when they sent King Charles I to the headsman.   And they stood against Cromwell himself and Presbyterian intolerance when Cromwell had won and come to power.   One of their poets (Milton) broke out in righteous indignation at the intolerance of the victors:

"New Presbyter is but old Priest writ large,"

and threw a challenge into their teeth:

"Dare ye for this adjure the civil sword,
To force our consciences, that Christ set free
And ride us with a classic hierarchy?"

They opposed Cromwell when he considered taking the throne and they cheered him when he refused it. They were fighting for a principle, not for any man. They were God's patriots more than England's.

They showered England with great men, great deeds, before they joined Particular and General branches into one, in 1891. They gave her the soldiers of her Revolution, her mighty men of peace; they provided Bunyan and his *Pilgrim's Progress*, written in Bedford jail; blind Milton and *Paradise Lost*, written in darkness; they produced Daniel Defoe and his *Robinson Crusoe*; Alexander McClaren and A. J. Gordon and Robert Hall and Spurgeon the Incomparable, preachers all. They gave England Andrew Fuller, in whose home was formed (in 1792) the English Baptist Missionary Society, and William Carey, the father of modern missions.

Let's divide the honors equally. Let's say that the Particular Baptists' greatest gift was Carey, who "has done more to make the India of today than Clive or Hastings, and contributed to the making of England hardly less than John Wesley" and that the General Baptists' greatest gift was Roger Williams, who contributed to the making of the United States hardly less than any dozen presidents.

Roger Williams was born with a tempest for a heart. From the cradle, he belonged, body and soul, to the Men-Who-Couldn't-And-Wouldn't-Fit-In. He graduated from Cambridge, brilliantly, and was sought by more than one good English parish when he took orders in the Church. He was a liberal churchman and a Separatist who boasted of it. That was his trouble; he never could keep things to himself. On a bleak fifth of February, 1631, he landed at Boston, after "a tempestuous voyage." He surely loved that trip, surely walked the deck in the gale with the rain on his face and the wild wind in his hair, peering ahead to where Boston was, wondering what he'd do there. Boston welcomed him with open arms, for he had a reputation; he was "a young minister, godly and zealous, having precious gifts." But he also had a mind of his own and a loose tongue with which to speak his mind. Hardly had he landed when he clashed with the Boston clergy; he advocated views quite out of sympathy with the ecclesiastical status quo. He refused to join the Boston church, for it was still too close, he thought, to the corruptions of the Church of England. Then the church at Salem called him and he accepted. But on the day he was to go, the Boston General Court interfered (which it had no right to do) and told the young rebel he couldn't stay in Salem. So he went on to Plymouth instead, where he preached for two years. He came to know some Indians there, some Narragansett chiefs and the Narragansett language.

In 1634 the church at Salem called him again and this time he went. Salem sat back and waited; this would be preaching worth listening to. It was. Soon Salem sat up and stared; this was explosive preaching, a theology charged with dynamite, dealing recklessly with Church and State and questioning the power of the Massachusetts police courts to deal with anything or anyone religious. The Boston Council got busy; John Cotton preferred charges. Yes, said Williams, the charges were true. He had said that the Puritans should have a patent from the Indians and not from the King for the land they lived on; he opposed wicked persons taking an oath, or praying, for these were acts of God's worship; he held that it was unlawful for the people to hear *any* of the ministers from the Parish assemblies of old England and that the power of the civil magistrates extended only "to the bodies, and goods, and outward state of men." What else, pray, could he think, or say? Outwardly, he wore the garb of a Puritan minister; inwardly, he was a Baptist.

The Salem church stood by him, but General Court had its way; Williams was exiled. The magistrates planned to ship him back to England; a ship rode at anchor in Boston Bay, ready for him. "But when they came at his house, they found he had been gone three days before; but whither they could not learn." He was three days deep in the forest, on his way to his old friends the Narragansett chiefs. From them he bought a strip of land at the mouth of the Mohassuck River, where he laid out a town. He named his town Providence. A good name, after his months in the forest. Soon his town was a town in fact, filled with sympathizers, rebels, malcontents, exiles, kindred spirits from Puritan towns, who drew up with him a "plantation covenant" under which all were mutually bound to "abide by the will of the majority," but only in "civil things." Williams' purpose in founding the colony, he said, was this: "I desired it might be for a shelter for persons distressed for conscience. I then considering the condition of divers of my distressed countrymen, I committed my said purchase to my loving friends. . . ." And he meant just that. He put the principle to work around Providence and showed the world, for the first time, that such a government and such an existence was not only possible, but more practical than any other. Doing that, he struck the first body blow at the theory of divine right, built a free government maintained solely on the rights and wishes of the governed, divorced completely Church and State, practiced the ideals of political and ecclesiastical liberty before they were taught in the schools of Europe. He was not only the founder of Providence and Rhode Island; he was "the most provocative figure thrown upon the Massachusetts shores by the upheaval in England, the one original thinker among a number of capable social architects"; he started a movement which rolled like a snowball through the early days of the Colonies, gaining weight and power, coming to rest at last in the first amendment to the Constitution of the United States!

He was not officially a Baptist when he came to Providence, but he soon took care of that. He had himself baptized by a Mr. Holliman, who had been a member of the Salem church; then he baptized Holliman and ten more. That was the first Baptist Church in America; but it was *not*, as many suppose, the "venerable mother Church of the American Baptists." No other churches sprang from that group at Providence; even Williams deserted them before he died. But that does not dim his glory as the pioneer in the fight for religious liberty in the United States; his insistence upon it made of it the first of the five principles laid down by the American Baptist and thrust it into the national Constitution as a national principle.

So dramatic is the figure of Roger Williams that we often miss another Rhode Island Baptist quite as important. Dr. John Clarke was a London physician who came to Boston just at the time of the fury aroused by Mistress Anne Hutchinson, that stormy petrel who dared discuss and criticize publicly the sermons of the

Puritan preachers and who professed a direct divine inspiration back of her piercing criticism. That was as bad, if not worse, than the heresy of Williams; out she went. Out, to Rhode Island, where Doctor Clarke offered her a home on land that Williams had purchased from the Indians, on Aquidneck Island, and a church to worship in, if she wanted it, at Newport. This church may or may not have been Baptist from the beginning; it certainly was by 1648, when it had fifteen members and Doctor Clarke as a "reading elder." He read well, gained popularity and was sent to England in 1651 to secure a charter for the colony. For twelve lonely years Clarke fought for that charter, and he was refused it until Charles II came to the throne in 1663; then he got a charter which declared that no person should "in anywise be molested, punished, disquieted or called in question for any differences of opinion in matters of religion," provided he kept the civil peace. Then Clarke came home, bowed to the applause of his friends, served two terms as deputy-governor of Rhode Island, retired to private life and died suddenly in 1676, fifteen years before the death of his old friend Roger Williams.

What Williams had started, Clarke had finished.

CHAPTER VI

THE BAPTISTS

(II)

DISTANCE loaned security to Roger Williams and John Clarke; the long arm of Massachusetts law was not long enough to reach from Boston to Providence. Had all Colonial Baptists settled with them in their free and happy Baptist commonwealth, they should *all* have been secure. But being Baptists, they could never do that. Their audacious principle, to live, must meet the enemy wherever the enemy is. And the enemy, just then, was in Massachusetts. So there they went, to purchase with blood and pain what the men of Newport and Providence had purchased for nothing.

Baptist facing Puritan! That was an irresistible force meeting an immovable object and great was the impact thereof. Thomas Painter of Hingham refused to have his child baptized; he was tied up and whipped. Henry Dunster, President of Harvard, and perhaps the finest president Harvard ever had, refused to have *his* child baptized, found himself thrust out of Cambridge, tried, convicted and admonished by the General Court. Only

his premature death saved him from worse.   John Clarke
(he of Newport) and Obadiah Holmes spent a Lord's
Day with a Baptist brother near Lynn, held a service at
the brother's house, were arrested and heavily fined, in
default of which they would be "well whipped."   A
sympathizer paid Clarke's fine, but Holmes was well
whipped, unmercifully beaten in a Boston street while
a sickened crowd looked on.   Holmes never flinched.
John Speer and John Hazel shook hands with him on
his way to the post and the handshake cost them forty
shillings apiece.   Stiff medicine, this, bitter gall.   It
should do the trick, should stamp out this Baptist non-
sense.   But something went wrong with the well-laid
Puritan plans.   With the gall at its bitterest, the Baptists
organized one church at Rehoboth, another at Boston.
Boston!   Like a foolish hen come to build her nest and
hatch her chicks next door to a nest of hawks!

Boston was flabbergasted and Boston was mad.
Boston swept down on the Baptist Church in the person
of a town constable, who nailed up the doors on the
heretics' meetinghouse and posted a notice thereon; the
Baptists were ". . . Inhibited to hold any meeting therein
or to open ye doors thereof. . . ."   They would, would
they?

Yes, they would.   The nails were pulled in just one
week and with them was pulled the power of the magistrates.   The Council had played its last card and it had

failed to win; it was the last serious Boston effort to halt the Baptists. The Puritan theocracy had broken down; the people were sick of whippings and banishments; in 1691 a new charter was granted by William and Mary, joining Massachusetts Bay and Plymouth into one colony, granting "liberty of conscience to all Christians, except Papists." It was more a measure of toleration than of liberty; the standing order continued until 1834.

Moving warily, carefully, gaining power as surely as a rolling snowball, the Baptists now spread their frontiers from the Boston hub. New York, after a short persecution under choleric old Peter Stuyvesant, soon had churches in New Amsterdam, Gravesend, Flushing, Oyster Bay. Things went handsomely in Pennsylvania; there was liberty for the Baptists here from the beginning, under Penn, and there was a consciousness of strength here which was lacking elsewhere. For mutual edification, "general meetings" were held in May and December; they were devotional meetings, evangelical; preachers came from New Jersey and New York. By 1707, official delegates were being sent and the first Baptist "Association" had been formed. Philadelphia became a natural center of Baptist interests and the "Association" was in a short while the most influential Baptist body in the Colonies, a position it never yielded. So influential was it that it designated, in 1742, the theology which was to typify the whole movement in

America; it wrote in that year a strongly *Calvinistic* confession of faith. That was a turning point, for heretofore the Baptists had been strongly Arminian in theology.

Things began to happen on the southern front at about this time. A law had been passed in Virginia setting a fine of two thousand pounds of tobacco on any parent who refused to have his children baptized. That law meant something; it was at first a cloud no bigger than a man's hand, but it grew rapidly into a storm which broke at last not only over Virginia, but over the whole nation.

At the dawn of the Great Awakening there were forty-seven Baptist Churches from Maine to Florida; all but seven of them were in the North. It was the weakest of the churches; there were not more than five hundred members altogether when Jonathan Edwards and George Whitefield were getting under way. With its evangelical emphasis, the Awakening offered a chance to any evangelical church, but the Baptists, strange to say, held aloof from it. Many of their churches closed their doors to Whitefield and the Tennents; the crowds went to the Congregationalists, to the Presbyterians. But the crowds came back! In spite of themselves, the Baptists found the Awakening a boon. Thousands of the converted found their old churches too cold, too unresponsive to their zeal and they turned to the Baptists as steel to a magnet. Out of the conflict between the "Old Lights" and "New Lights" came a new sect, the *Separate* Baptists. Not all of those who separated themselves from the old churches became Baptists, but enough of them to make the once despised baptizers a force to be handled carefully. Those old Baptists who had stood out against the revivals of the Awakening called themselves *Regular* Baptists, to distinguish themselves from their brethren among the Separatists.

The Separate Baptists tore the South from the Episcopalians at the very moment when the Colonies were being torn from the Crown. The Continental Armies marched from '75 to '81; the Baptist struggle for equality and recognition was at its fiercest, in Virginia, from '75 to '99. They had entered Virginia in force in 1714, to run immediately afoul of grim opposition by the Episcopalians. The assault on them by the Established Church of the South is the blackest blot on the record of any church in America, and the most inexcusable of all Colonial history. From the granting of the original charter of 1606, which "compelled worship" according to the rites and doctrines of the Church of England, through the awful laws of Berkeley to the hour of the meeting of the First Congress, the Baptists were hounded from one jail to the next, dragged from whipping-post to dungeon without rest or respite. William Weber and Joseph Anthony were locked up in Chesterfield County jail and told to keep quiet. They preached through the bars of their cells to crowds in the streets outside. John Waller, Louis Craig and James Childs were mobbed and brought into court, where a wild-eyed prosecuting attorney cried above the hubbub, "May it please your worship, these men are great disturbers of the peace; they cannot meet a man upon the road, but they must ram a text of scripture down his throat!"

It looked bad for the defendants. Fifty miles away, a young Scotch-American lawyer named Patrick Henry (a good Episcopalian) heard of it, turned red to the roots of his hair, saddled his horse and galloped into town. Waving the indictment above his head in a fury wilder than that of the prosecuting attorney, he roared, "For preaching the gospel of God. Great God! Great God!! Great God!!!" (He said the same thing, years later, in a slightly different phrase: "Give me liberty, or give me death.") The preachers were acquitted.

More Baptists came to court as the fight dragged on and more were acquitted. Their persistence and fortitude won attention, sympathy, co-operation. James Madison came over to their side; a man named Jefferson, living at Monticello, stopped, looked, listened and said the Baptists were right. A country squire named Washington, living at Mount Vernon, was impressed.

Sympathy in such quarters helped turn the tide. In 1779, the Virginia legislature stopped forever the taxing of Virginians for the support of an established clergy. That was a hard blow for the Established Church; it tottered, it fell, and as it fell the Baptists rose. Then Jefferson wrote "An Act for Establishing Religious Freedom" and Madison took the stump for it; in 1786 the Act became a law. Virginia has given us presidents; she is "the mother of presidents." But when she passed that law in 1786, which established absolute separation between Church and State by act of government, she made "the greatest distinctive contribution of America to the sum of Western civilization." Virginia did that? Or the Virginia Baptist?

The victory in Virginia was a transfusion of new blood into Baptist veins. It was followed by another. The Revolution raised havoc with the Episcopalians and nearly destroyed the Methodists, but it helped make the Baptists. That was only fair, for the Baptists had been helping to make the Revolution. Some observers (they may be Baptist observers) claim that the Baptists were loyal to a man, that there was not a single Baptist Tory to be found; others admit there were a few, hard to find. Whoever is right, Washington himself told them that they had been "uniformly and almost unanimously, the firm friend to civil liberty and the preserving promoters of our glorious Revolution." That they supported it at all is source for wonder and proof of their Christianity. Not only in fighting it did they turn the other cheek after the jailings and the whippings of Massachusetts and Virginia, but they went farther; they loved their former enemies well enough to die with them on Hessian bayonets. Their principle had conquered again; their devotion to the cause of freedom had caused them to forget old scars, old grudges. A spirit like that could inspire only respect and tolerance. When the war was over, the Baptists couldn't recognize themselves. They were dressed up in brand new clothes. *Before* the war, they had been small, persecuted groups; *after* it, they were wealthy and influential as well as respected for writing their principles into the law of the land. They were numerous and aggressive and they had an appeal particularly attractive to the common man, who was right then on his way to high places.

They did not rest in the flush of victory; they were not so foolish as to believe that this new nation of theirs was safe for democracy even with the British gone and the Established Church in a state of collapse. The states had as yet to band themselves into a Union; the Constitution was the next step. Presented to the several states for ratification, the Constitution met troubled waters. The Baptists didn't just like that document, for it said nothing of the separation of Church and State. But it was better than none, so they supported it and voted for it. In many states, it was adopted only on the promise that an amendment on religious freedom would be added after adoption. Even with that promise, ratification was doubtful. The states were jealous of one another, dubious of centralized Federal power. Finally, Massachusetts and Virginia became the pivotal states in the fight; they must pass it, or the whole thing would be lost. Massachusetts fell into line with an early election and that left Virginia. Now Madison was running for the state legislature of Virginia against a Baptist Elder, John Leland, in Orange County. Madison's presence in that body was necessary to ratify the Constitution and Madison was beaten before the election! Orange was overwhelmingly Baptist; Madison hadn't a chance. Leland knew that. He also knew that without Madison's golden voice and political influence, there would be no Constitution. So, with victory already in his hand, he dropped out of the race and gave Madison an open road. The rest is history. We call James Madison the "Father of the Constitution." But is he? What shall we do with Elder Leland?

Meanwhile, Baptists everywhere kept talking about that Amendment. A General Committee of the Baptists in Virginia met in 1788 to discuss "whether the new Constitution . . . made sufficient provision for the secure enjoyment of religious liberty." They talked it over among themselves and they talked it over with

Mr. Madison and they sent a delegation up to talk it over with Mr. Washington, who was now President Washington. Their reception was cordial, sympathetic. So sympathetic that the Congress, urged on by the President, made it their first business to consider what the Baptists had to say. The first line of the first Amendment, therefore, reads: "Congress shall make no law respecting an establishment of religion, or prohibiting the free exercise thereof. . . ."

It was done. Forever done. Never again shall we have to fight that fight. It was fought for us by the followers of Williams and Clarke; their sons, ten million strong, will see that the works of their fathers will not be lost.

At midnight of January 1, 1800, the Baptists had eleven hundred churches and one hundred thousand members. They had not a single State Convention such as exists today. They were divided into Regular, Free Will, Seventh Day and Sixth Principle Baptists, with no denominational organization to unite them save a few scattered "Associations." Ten of these associations were distinctly anti-missionary in attitude. They had been growing fast; so many new members had crowded into their house that the walls seemed ready to burst for lack of room. There they stood, on the eve of the era of expansion, with the country on tiptoe for the push to the West, for all the world like a great gawky youngster

who had suddenly, unaccountably become a man, quite
unaware of his own strength. Or like a great newly
recruited army scattered in unconnected camps. What
they needed, that midnight, was a solidifying, a binding
power. They found it.

In 1812, while that grand old man-o'-war, *The Constitution,* was searching the seas for the British *Guerrière,*
two humble little passenger ships were plowing the seas
toward India, with the first of the modern army of
American missionaries on their decks. Adoniram Judson
and Luther Rice, haystack volunteers, were on their
way to Calcutta. In Calcutta they became Baptists and
Rice returned home to tell the Baptists about it and to
gain their support. He toured the country, poking the
old fires of neglected missionary passion; he had a good
story and he knew how to tell it. The Baptists came
out of their "anti" attitude, backed him, sent him flying
back to Calcutta to tell Judson to go ahead. He stirred
up or created missionary societies all over the country
and gave the Baptists a common cause; for the first time,
the young giant of the denominations was to realize his
power. "When revolution is brewing at home," said
a wise French king, "stir up a war abroad." That's
what had happened to the Baptists, at the hands of
Luther Rice.

By 1814, the General Convention of the Baptist Denomination in the United States for Foreign Missions

(a big name, but it was a big organization!) was at work. It met once in three years; hence, people called it the "Triennial Convention." Much good came out of Triennial; not only a Foreign Missions Society, but one for Home Missions too, a Baptist Publication Society, an American Baptist Historical Society, an Educational Society and a Baptist Young People's Union. Just for variety, it established a few theological seminaries. Triennial was a loose uniting bond, giving rhyme and reason to the Baptist effort; it was a drum, on which they pounded the step, the beat, the cadence for their march; it created the denominational consciousness so sorely needed.

The march now turned westward, following the leaping frontier. In truth, the Baptist led the frontiersman. Sulphuric Daniel Boone, that wild man of the western No-Man's Land, had a brother, one "Squire" Boone, who was a Baptist preacher; the mother of young Abe Lincoln was a staunch Baptist and his father helped to build the Baptist Church at Pigeon Creek. Into the wilderness, into the boisterous pandemonium of the wilderness town, rode the Baptist on horseback. Call the roll of the new states (Kentucky, Ohio, Indiana, Illinois, Iowa, Texas, California, Colorado, Oregon) and find a Baptist at work preaching God and building his meetinghouse. No spot was too hard to reach, no town too tough to tackle. Was there drinking and carousing, fighting, gambling, killing, horse-stealing or (which was worse) horse-racing? He fought it, tempered it with his stern code, stood for law and order if he had to stand alone, took the snap, the sting, the poison out of it. When he dropped on the wilderness trail, the churches he'd left behind him carried on.

"Robert Hicklin," says the church book of old South Elkhorn Church, Kentucky, "was excluded from the church for horse-racing." Or, "A charge was brought against Sister Polly Edrington for . . . Indeavouring by tatteling to set several of the neighbors at strife with each other. She was excluded for the same." They "also excluded Molly, a black member formerly belonging to William Fitzgerald, for telling lies." But this frontier Baptist congregation was merciful when confronted by honest contrition: Sister Arnett, of Mt. Tabor Church, Kentucky, was cited for drinking. She "appeared to be humble, and very sorry for what she had done, therefore, the Church restore(d) her to fellowship."

It took one hundred years to win the frontier, to possess the West from the Alleghenies to the Pacific. Could it have been won at all without the aid of the circuit-rider? Crude as he was, at times, illiterate and unclean, lips stained with tobacco and tongue thick with white liquor, he was nevertheless the saving salt of the whole situation. He drew the fangs of the rattlesnake-sin of the frontier and got it ready for democracy by establishing that sense of equality which at last took Old Hickory Jackson to the White House.

Even this brilliant period of growth and accomplishment had its bad spots. Some of the sheep got to straying from the fold. From 1825 to 1865, there was a mighty exodus from the main bodies out into smaller sects, an exodus, however, which failed to halt the larger church. The greatest achievement of the Baptists for the century was their triumph over the wave of disastrous, destructive and divisive movements which threatened them. There were the Hardshell and Campbell movements, the division into northern and southern Baptists, and the Civil War. Logically, the Baptists should have been shattered by one or the other; actually, they grew stronger than ever. The Hardshell movement (they expounded a stricter Calvinistic theology) and the Campbellites (who held different views on conversion, baptism, etc.,) took a cool two hundred thousand members away from the parent Church; yet in 1845 that parent Church showed a gain of one hundred and twenty-six per cent in the South, of one hundred and seventy-five per cent in the nation as a whole!

Eighteen hundred and forty-five! That was the year when the great split came over slavery. The year before, a pronouncement came in General Convention to the effect that, "If anyone who should offer himself for a missionary, having slaves, should insist on retaining them as his property, we could not appoint him." That was the end, for the southerners. They withdrew, in May of 1845, and founded their Southern Baptist Convention. Would God that great split could have been avoided! Would God the whole ghastly error of the Civil War could have been avoided! It should never have been fought. But it was, and for thirty years thereafter the South lay prostrate in the dust. But look at this: by 1880, there were 1,672,631 Baptists in the South, over two and one half millions in all the United States. A solid million gained in the South, in spite of the war, and 1,337,399 new members gained North and South!

The division of the Baptists into northern and southern groups still stands. While efforts at reunion have come to nothing, there is absolute agreement in doctrine between the two and members are transferred without question in an unrestricted amity. That amity began soon after Grant and Lee shook hands and went home, after Appomattox. Almost at once, as time flies, the Baptists went to work to relieve the real victim of the war. That victim was the Negro. Far from being the benefactor he was intended to be, the black stood at the surrender like a youngster toying with a precious Venetian vase. He had freedom, but he didn't know what to do with it.   Carefully the Baptists guided him, in the finest piece of home missionary work in the annals of the Church.   They built schools, churches, institutions of all kinds, for his own particular benefit. Some day someone will write a great story—the story of the Christianizing of the Negro in the days of slavery and afterward.   And the Baptists will be among the great heroes of the story.   Education, they saw, was the remedy and the safeguard against the perils of the liberation; religious education, or education with a religious aim.   They have outstripped all others in the building of colored schools; in the year of our Lord 1936, the Colored Baptists have a membership of three and one half millions and twenty-three thousand churches.

That religious education was by no means restricted to the South or to this period.   The Baptist has always been an educator.   In admiring his stand on Church-and-State, we often forget that; we shouldn't, for he has given us too much.   He has led the way, from the beginning, in the Sunday-School movement.   Robert Raikes, commonly credited with starting it, really started a school which met on Sundays, with paid teachers, for the instruction of the children of the poor in secular as well as religious subjects; the first school in history for the popular study of the Bible by youth was set up in London by a wealthy Baptist deacon, William Fox, in 1783.   By 1785, Fox and his Baptist aides had launched their movement on a broader scale, and called it "The Society for the Support and Encouragement of Sunday Schools." The first Sunday School in America, dealing strictly in *religious* education, was founded at the First Baptist Church of Philadelphia in 1815. The first Sunday-School paper for young people in the United States, the *Young Reaper,* was a Baptist production. So were the International Uniform Sunday-School Lessons, which were the work of a Chicago Layman, B. F. Jacobs.

Just to make sure that youth would stay in the Church after Sunday-School days were past, a Baptist Young People's Union (The B. Y. P. U.) was organized in 1891. It rivals Christian Endeavor with a million members.

Then things took another turn. That distinguished European, Visser 't Hooft, holds that "the social movement in the Church is the distinguishing characteristic of American Christianity"; one might add that the Baptists have been particularly distinguished in the social movement. The Jeremiah of the Christian social movement in this country was saintly, Baptist, burning Rauschenbusch of Rochester, who knew humanity and therefore loved it, who sat up all night reading books on child labor and went into his classes next morning to drive the piteous cry of the children like white-hot nails into the hearts of his students. And there was

Doctor Vedder, who told the terrible tale with his ir-
refutable historian's logic, who made it so clear that
God's will had to be done among the men of earth as
well as among the angels of heaven. Thousands of Baptists have followed Rauschenbusch and Vedder in the
fight for social and economic justice which has marked
the present century. In 1914 they were granted high
honors by being named in the yearbook of the American
Brewers' Association as one of the chief enemies of the
brewmaster and his brew; in 1924, with their churches
full of memorial plaques from the World War, they
swung an official uppercut at Mars with the declaration
that ". . . the Church must not only condemn war, but
must take an active part in discussing and promoting
the things that make for peace." A complete about-
face, this position on war; a man of snap judgment
might conclude that the Baptists, even yet, know not
their own minds.

But they do. The Baptist knows his own mind and
he has an embarrassing habit of speaking it, quite
plainly, when it comes time to speak. He's changeable,
yes; what else could he be, in view of his preaching of
individual freedom and thought? He's a breed without,
beyond the law; he's an irregular, a reckless, restless
irregular who cannot and will not fit in. Contradictions?
He's full of them; they are moral muscle over his
spiritual bone. The Baptists have been patriots, making

their homes and digging their graves wherever freedom was denied; they held up the hands of Cromwell and Washington as Hur held up the hands of Moses; they have entered regiments in scores of wars; they sent Sir Henry Havelock to the relief of Lucknow and they sent Sam Houston to Texas; yet had Cromwell or Washington or Sir Henry or Sam Houston denied God in the interests of the State, the Baptists would have denied them and their lower patriotism at a moment's notice. They have denied the State, time and time again, for a higher loyalty to the Kingdom of God, for a higher patriotism. That's contradiction; we need it. With an anti-missions sentiment strong in certain of their churches, they gave the world Carey and Judson and Rice. Denying infant baptism, they gave us the Sunday School! With many in their ranks suspicious of education, they have presented us with seventy-nine colleges (Bates, Brown, Bucknell, Chicago, Colby, Colgate, Denison, Franklin, Vassar), two hundred and fifty (plus) universities and secondary schools and ten seminaries. They have more dollars invested in education, at the moment, than any other church in America. Lovers of simplicity in worship, they have produced an uncounted army of sweet singers in Israel; from the Baptists (can any other church match this?) came *Blessed Be the Tie That Binds; The Morning Light Is Breaking; America; Majestic Sweetness Sits Enthroned;*

On Jordan's Stormy Banks I Stand; Come Thou Font of Every Blessing; Oh, Could I Speak the Matchless Worth; Awake, My Soul; How Firm a Foundation; My Hope Is Built on Nothing Less; Hold the Fort; All Hail the Power of Jesus' Name; Saviour, Thy Dying Love; Holy, Holy, Holy; Shall We Gather at the River; He Leadeth Me; I Need Thee Every Hour. If this be contradiction, make the most of it.

They have the strength of numbers. In 1800 they had one hundred thousand; in 1850 they were eight hundred and fifteen thousand. In 1900 they numbered over five millions, in 1934, ten millions. That represents power. Power to grow. Power to do things. Power that came to them by no freak of historical chance, but because they had (and still have) the most popular idea in the world and the most effective method of putting it across. They insist upon freedom; utter, absolute freedom. They get it by appealing to the masses instead of the classes, to those who need it most and who will fight hardest to get it. They have never longed for the toga of the State; they have grown up in log cabins and small-town jails; they have a long and honorable record of ministry to the sick, of succor to the lowly. No wonder they have eleven million members around the world. We may as well command the sun to stand still as to command a church like that to stop growing.

The world has done its best to stop them; we can trace their history more readily in the bloody footprints of their martyrs than in the ink of their historians. We have tried to shame them by whipping them and they have made us ashamed of our whipping-posts. We chained them in jail and discovered that the other end of the chain was fast about our own necks. We let their blood in Boston and the South, only to find the fairest American flowers we know growing from that very soil. Addlepated world! You tried to stamp them out and all you got for it was to have them leave their stamp on you!

THE PRESBYTERIANS

CHAPTER VII

THE PRESBYTERIANS

(I)

ALL roads in Europe lead to Geneva; she is a junior
Colossus straddling the highway from Paris to Rome, a
long road worn smooth by the feet of the great. Today
the legates of princes, potentates and presidents arrive
in style and fanfare to weave around their League-of-
Nations' council table the varicolored strands of international destinies. Yesterday, and earlier than
yesterday, the refugees of kings and popes swung up that
road, without fanfare and in anything but style, seeking
with furtive eye a spot where they might lay their
weary heads. Yesterday, today and forever the city of
Geneva is a city of confusion and the abiding-place of
hope.

Up the road, in 1530, came a little French lawyer in
a hurry, fleeing persecution in Italy for what he hoped
might be sanctuary in Germany. That is, he had been
trained for the law in France, but he had turned to
theology. Jean Cauvin, embryo lawyer, became John
Calvin, theologian. He couldn't stay long in Geneva;

he must get on, must put more miles between himself and the Vatican. He could only rest overnight at the home of William Farel, a brother Frenchman and a sword-swinging reformer who had just driven back the troops of Catholic Savoy and made Geneva independent and Protestant. And undecided. What to do now, William Farel, with your newly liberated city? You had no Catholics, neither had you any government nor any strong hand to lay a worthy keel for your new ship of state. Said Farel to keen-eyed Calvin, "Stay to build here a city for God." Said Calvin to Farel, "I go on in the morning." He had studying to do in Germany, books to read, books to write, things to think out. He was only twenty-seven, a young man in a young man's world. "Put forward your studies as a pretext if you will," thundered Farel, "but if you refuse this work, the curse of God will rest upon you." Back and forth they argued it, pro and con before the crackling fire on Farel's hearth, playing battledore and shuttlecock with Geneva and the world. Farel won the argument. Calvin stayed. Calvin reached out with his long, thin, scholar's fingers and took hold of the city as a potter takes hold of a lump of clay. He molded Geneva; he was halted in his molding by banishment, but returned to mold again, to reform, reshape, remake it into a town for us to imitate. His fingers were firm and the will behind the fingers knew no variableness nor turning;

the clay either conformed, or he cast its unconforming parts away; the Genevans either bowed to Calvin, or took the road for Italy or France. He burned Servetus and he hanged another; he burned thirty-four other objectors and he filled the city jail with more who couldn't agree. He seldom smiled. He was almost ascetic. He was as cold as the summit of Jungfrau. He sat stiffly straight in his chair and his eyes bored through you. He was "God's prosecuting attorney." He wore a black gown. A black Geneva gown.

Burnings and hangings and jailings notwithstanding, he got what he wanted and he gave Geneva and Europe and Protestantism what they had to have to live: stability and organization. When Calvin was done with Geneva, says Macaulay, Geneva was "the cleanest and most wholesome city in Europe." That was because Geneva now had the cleanest, most wholesome faith in God. Calvin based the whole Genevan adventure on God and God alone. He fought first of all to replace the inefficient law of Geneva with the stable law of God. The Sovereignty of God! There you have Calvinism, and the Presbyterianism that grew out of Calvinism, in a nutshell. God in His glory rules the world; God dominates our thinking, feeling, doing, our every personal, social, economic, political, religious relationship. We must, said Calvin, be solely dependent on Him, must without reserve believe in Him, must have faith in His goodness however it works out with us. Without Him, we can do nothing; left to himself, man is totally depraved and can do nothing to save himself. (This is the doctrine of total depravity.) Our saving rests entirely with God. He elects, chooses, to save some; all others are lost. God willed it that way, predestined it so. (This is the doctrine of predestination.) God's power and will are irresistible. But His grace is also irresistible; nothing, no one, can halt or delay it. The saved are saved in spite of themselves and the lost are lost by the same token. Under this sovereignty, the elect and the damned have certain rights, certain duties to perform. Man is the co-signer of a spiritual covenant or contract with the Father. Rousseau the Frenchman talked much of a *social* contract between man and man, of which all of us, willy-nilly, were a part. Calvin put it on higher ground when he made it a covenant between man and God. And Rousseau, who seldom slapped the back of any priest or preacher, thought enough of John Calvin to hold that "whatever revolutions time may bring in our religion, as long as love of country, and liberty, is not extinct among us, the memory of that great man will be held in reverence." Fools call Calvin a burning bigot; scholars know him as a Man of Destiny. No man ever did more for human intelligence and education in school and college, for an intelligent ministry, for the earth's religiously oppressed, for a sane theory of Church and State and for a system of theology which has bred a race of heroes.

There were other sovereignties in the Calvinistic system: the sovereignty of Christ in salvation, the sovereignty of the Scriptures in faith and conduct, the sovereignty of the individual conscience in the interpretation of God's will. . . . These, with the basic belief in the sovereignty of God, form the background of Calvinism and the groundwork of Presbyterianism; out of them, as the oak out of the acorn, grew a new phase in the cycle of this world's life. Out of it all sprouted a new economics. Calvin rejected the old laws of interest and usury. That is, he recognized, officially, that these laws were passé; they had been disregarded and broken for years; feudalism had long been a cripple on its last legs. All Calvin did was to recognize its state of total depravity and plan a new economics to take its place. That new economics was capitalism. Calvin did not invent capitalism; he gave it a religious note and a moral or ethical sanction. And if the capitalists of subsequent years had used and not abused his moral and ethical and religious precepts, their capitalism would not be the weird wreck it is today.

A new politics leaped from the loins of Calvinism; in his system was the taproot of democracy. The government he gave Geneva was Europe's first government of the people, by the people, for the people, and it has not perished from the earth. His was, at bottom, a bourgeois movement. It snubbed the kings and enthroned the common man. "Called of God and heir of heaven," says Greene the historian, "the trader at his counter and the digger of the field rose into equality with the noble and the king." It was a representative government, through which the people ruled themselves, their State and their Church. It was composed of a majority of laymen and a minority of preachers; they were called "*presbuteroi*," ("elders," or "aldermen") and the Genevan Protestant Church became the *Presbyterian* Church.

Church and State were separate in a novel way: the Church was put above the State and the State was bound to enforce the rulings and penalties of the Church. And the Church saw to it that she covered just about everything; she held authority over the least detail in the life of the least of her members. But her rule was democratic, through a council, for all that; democratic, or "presbyterian," in the hands of the chosen elders of the people.

This new form of church polity was as revolutionary as the new form of political government. It was and is a middle-of-the-road position running between episcopacy and congregationalism and making use of the best features of both. There are no bishops or cardinals or popes, but only moderators, with most limited powers.

Each church is ruled by presbyters, or elders; grouped into conciliar courts, these rule the whole of the united Church. That is their *presbyterian* system, from which they take their name. They take their faith and theology from Calvin, emphasizing divine sovereignty and free grace and offering salvation not by rite or ceremony, but solely on the unmerited grace of God. It is a church of the people. It is a church with a covenant.

Naturally, the world was interested in all this. "If a man make . . . a better mousetrap than his neighbor," says Emerson, "though he build his home in the woods, the world will make a beaten path to his door." The world beat a path to Calvin's door, for he had created something. He had put the ideology of the Reformation to work. Luther had laid down the principles and Calvin had applied them to government and society. Calvin did not, strictly, found the Presbyterian Church; he expanded and practiced the principles which, in other countries (Switzerland, Holland, England, Scotland, Ireland, France) developed into Presbyterianism. The flocking to him of the religious leaders of every State in Europe made him, unwittingly, the only international reformer. They came to him from France, where Rome still ruled. By 1560 there were two thousand churches of Presbyterian persuasion in France. The French Protestant called himself a Huguenot ("oath companion") and he wrote his protest in blood. A bell rang in the tower of St.

Germain l'Auxerrois one hideous night in 1572, the signal for the slaughter of fifty thousand Huguenots in a space of thirty days. War and massacre followed war and massacre between Protestant and Catholic until Henry IV signed the Edict of Nantes, granting religious protection to all. But Louis XIV undid Henry's Act by repealing it, in 1685, and the Huguenots left France by the thousand. Some three to four hundred thousand got away; as many more were caught and sent to dungeons or the galleys. Many turned west, across the Atlantic. To New York and Maryland. To Virginia and South Carolina.

The black Genevan gown slipped in behind the dikes of Holland and gave a Presbyterian tinge to the Dutch Reformed Church. ("Presbyterian" and "Reformed" are quite synonymous.) From Holland and Germany it came on to New York and Pennsylvania. And it invaded England. Protestants running from Bloody Mary's Catholic reaction came to Geneva and went back to England with Geneva Bibles and Calvin's theology. Calvinism became the very heart of Puritanism; the Calvinists led in the fight first against the Pope and then against the King, rolled the head of Charles I in Cromwell's basket and came by the thousand to settle New England.

But it was not in the conflicts of France or Holland or Germany or even England that the fathers of American

Presbyterianism were born, but in those of Scotland and
Ireland. The black gown started for America with those
"godly bands" of Scots, holding to the principles of the
Reformed Church, refusing to bow their necks or warp
their souls to the standards of the King or the Pope and
flying as outlaws before the wrath of both. Nobles and
people alike joined in a covenant to aid each other in the
defense of their religious rights and fled together into
the hills to hold their services when they found themselves driven out of their churches. They prayed in
hidden crags and fens, sang their Psalms in obscure lochs
and glens. Brave old elders stood up in the quiet forest
and begged God with trembling voices to protect them
from the minions of Pope and King who hunted them
like animals; they dared not sing too loud, lest their
enemies hear and come; fair ladies sat sidesaddle on their
horses, ready to run at the signal of the sentinel who
watched over them from the nearby hilltop. "Covenanters," they called themselves. Caught between
Pope and King, they preferred to die rather than sell
their souls; scores of them were killed in their hills and
buried there and their graves grew wild with brambles
in a thousand hidden dells. Sir Walter Scott knew these
Covenanters; he wrote of one of them, a fine old
saint called Old Mortality, who went about the dells
scraping away the bramble and cutting afresh, through
the moss and decay, the names of those who had so

gloriously died.   A labor of love, for Old Mortality, but God had already immortalized them; He had made of the Covenanters the seed of the Presbyterian Church in the United States, the stepping-stone of the Presbyterians across the ocean from Scotland and Geneva to New York.

They were a determined lot, the Covenanters.   When they made up their minds to a thing, that thing had to be.   They made up their minds that music and statuary and ritual and hymn-singing and the art of the Roman Church were not for them nor for their services; so out went the art, the music, the ritual; crucifixes were torn from their niches and Madonnas were burned and rose windows were smashed.   That didn't leave them much to work with . . . only the Book of Psalms to sing from and a stern preacher to listen to.   They sang those Psalms without musical accompaniment.   (Their lineal descendant in the United States, the Reformed Presbyterian Church, still does that!)   They became sermon experts.   Creeds and formulas and articles of faith took the place of the lost Madonnas and rose windows; Scotland was one great school, debating, evaluating, developing religious faith.   They fought on doggedly, and waited patiently for some great leader to come, to lead them back to their churches.   He came.   He was John Knox.

Knox knew Scotland.   He had ranged it with Master George Wishart, preacher, who had exhorted men to

God in a black mantle which reached to his shoe-tops, with white cuffs and a white band about his neck, rousing the ire of Rome's man in Scotland, Cardinal Beaton. With him, on his tours, went young John Knox. When the Cardinal's henchmen seized Master Wishart and carried him off to burn him at the stake, Wishart kissed his executioner on the cheek, but he shouted at Beaton: "Look at yonder proud man! I tell you that in a brief space ye shall see him flung out on yonder ramparts with infamy and scorn equal to the pomp and dignity with which he now occupies it." It came about just that way; before Wishart's ashes had been blown to the four winds, fifteen avengers had broken into the Castle of St. Andrews and murdered the Cardinal. Knox called it "a Godly act." Knox was trapped with the killers in the Castle, captured and sent to the galleys. For nineteen months he was chained to an oar; he pulled to the crack of the master's gavel and he thought he was doomed to die right there. But one fine day the master unlocked his chain; he'd been pardoned, by intercession of King Edward the Sixth. He stepped from the galley to the court of the King, where he performed the duties of King's chaplain and made three fast friends: Cranmer, Latimer and Ridley.

One day he climbed the long hill to Geneva and looked into the eyes of John Calvin. Two of the world's giants, face to face. Fire meeting fire. Calvin talked with him.

Calvin taught him.   Calvin inspired him.   The voice of
Calvin sent him back to fight for Scotland as the voice
of the Master had sent Peter back to fight for Rome; he
threw his black gown across his shoulders and started for
Edinburgh.

The instant his foot touched Scottish soil the lightning
flashed and the fight was on.   Knox fought so well that his
Scots were able to proclaim the Reformed faith as the
faith of their State within a year after his return; if they
cheered for that, they cheered too soon.   It was a
chimerical victory, for it was upset immediately by the
accession to the throne of Mary, who called herself Mary
Queen of Scots, who was the French and Catholic
daughter of the Guise, French Mary of Lorraine.   Knox
despised her as he despised her Church and set himself
against her.   He threw theological vitriol in the face of
the Pope at long range and defiance in the face of Mary
from the foot of her throne.   Was she not Catholic and
was not that enough?   Would she not make Scotland
Catholic, if she could?   He preached at St. Giles, calling
Mary to account as he would have called the least subject
of her realm, excoriating her Church and bitterly condemning her for her marriage to Lord Darnley.   Mary
commanded him to hold his peace.   "Madame," replied
John Knox, "in matters of conscience and religion I have
never feared the face of clay, though that face belonged
to a Queen."   Bold words to speak in public.   In his

private prayers, he was equally determined: "Great God," he sobbed, "give me Scotland, or I die." The people waited with their hearts in their mouths to see whether Scotland would fall to the French Queen or the preacher of St. Giles. Scotland was burning.

Mary settled the issue herself, after years of blood. Darnley was murdered; the finger of suspicion pointed to the Queen. In the face of this, she married an old lover, the Earl of Bothwell, a rough man and licentious, but a brave one at that; and she married him under the rites of the Protestant Church. That turned both Catholic and Protestant against her and together they drove her from the land. She abdicated and escaped. Escaped to England, where Elizabeth shut her up for twenty years and then sent her to the block.

Knox had won. Scotland was Protestant, Presbyterian. In the flush of triumph he preached the coronation sermon of James I, Mary's son, in 1567; five years later, just after hearing of St. Bartholomew's, he died, certain that at last the land of the heather was free. But the land of the heather was not free. James I and Charles I made up their minds (why?) that while Scotland might be Protestant, it would bow its neck to the Stuart Church of England; in 1637 Archbishop Laud announced that thereafter the clergy of Edinburgh would recite the services of the English Prayer Book. The Archbishop himself came to town to see that it was done; he came to old St. Giles and found himself faced by a screaming mob. As he entered the church he was greeted with cries of "Stone him!" "Baal!" "Antichrist!" As the Dean rose to start reading, someone flung a stool at his head. Jenny Geddes flung that stool; Jenny Geddes, who kept a green stall in the High Street and who was, though she never knew it, ancestress to one Sir Auckland Geddes, sometime British Ambassador to the United States. The riot of which Jenny was a part spread from St. Giles across the city and across Scotland and it ended only when the last trace of Episcopacy was gone out of Scotland. That was in 1643, when a "Solemn League and Covenant" was drawn up to give Scotland a democratic government and a united religious faith. It was signed by both Houses of Parliament, by the Universities and by the Westminster Assembly of Divines.

That Westminster Assembly was a landmark in Presbyterian history; it was called by Parliament and it was composed of one hundred and twenty-one ministers, ten peers, twenty members of the House of Commons and a delegation of Scots. Before the Scots arrived, it was just another assembly, called for the high-sounding duty of "the settling of the government and the liturgy of the Church of England." It hardly accomplished that; but with the aid of the Scots, who sat down resolved to have "no bishops and no king," it did something which

was even more important. It created a Westminster
Confession of Faith which was the most clearly defined
of all previous Protestant documents and which put in
concrete form the faith of the Presbyterian for centuries
to come. It was a stately presentation of the Calvinistic
position; it is today the official symbol of Anglo-Saxon
Presbyterianism, in Scotland, in England, in Ireland, in
America.

Parliament approved of the work of the Westminster
Divines, adopted their suggestions and England was officially Presbyterian for a few following years. They
proved to be troubled years, years of error. Religious
issues became political issues; denominations became
political parties. Episcopalians were Royalists and Presbyterians were Parliamentarians. Bad business, that.
Bad for English Presbyterianism, at any rate. Pure
politics lifted them to power and pure politics, in the
end, hurled them down again. As a State Church, the
Presbyterians were a failure; when Cromwell died and
the kings came back, the last remnant of their power was
torn from them. The returned monarchy drove them
out of England and across the Scottish moors, where the
"Covenanters" roused again, signed their names to yet
more sacred compacts, with their own blood on pin-
points, to stand to the death against Roman bishops and
English kings.

Meanwhile, a migration had been going on. While

the Puritans were settling Massachusetts, the Scotch were settling Ulster, in Ireland. Scots, in Ireland. That made them "Scotch-Irish"; Presbyterian Scotch-Irish, in a most inhospitable land. Had they stayed at home, we might never have seen them in America, nor known them as one of the great molding forces of our land. But they went to Ireland. And they got into trouble in Ireland, with more Episcopalians and more Roman Catholics. Dragoons dispersed their presbyteries, armed mobs chased them from their churches; they were told to "get out or get in line." Tell a Scotchman that and he'll get out. Many of them stood to fight and the old scenes of the Covenanter fight in Scotland were repeated; many more, reaching the end of patience, slipped away to America, where a man could worship at his chosen altar without soldiers pounding on the door. They came in shiploads, in droves, and they filtered into the Middle Atlantic States. On one of their crowded ships came a preacher, Francis Makemie.

Now Makemie was not the first Scotch-Irish preacher to display the black Geneva gown in America. There were many before him. There were at least four thousand Presbyterians from England, Scotland and Ireland in this country by 1640. The Church in New England, for instance, has been aptly described as a "Congregationalized Presbyterianism, or a Presbyterianized Congregationalism." John Eliot was a Presbyterian before he went Congregationalist. Richard Salwey was one of the earliest Presbyterian preachers; John Young was exhorting for Calvinism on Long Island in 1641; Abraham Pierson was working in New Jersey; Francis Doughty, English refugee, was in Taunton, Massachusetts, and is said to have been the first Presbyterian preacher in New York City. Richard Denton organized the church at Hempstead, Long Island, and the Hempsteaders stoutly defend their claim that their church is the oldest "of the *denomination* which has always been called Presbyterian" on this side of the Atlantic. Matthew Hill labored in Maryland; so did Colonel Beale. These two, with the help of Francis Doughty (who moved down to Maryland when he ran afoul of Peter Stuyvesant in New York) were the real founders of Presbyterianism in the Middle States.

But it took Francis Makemie to bind together these scattered churches, as Muhlenberg had bound the Lutherans. Makemie liked his job and he liked America, which was more than we can say for some others who sailed quickly back when they found what they were up against. Makemie looked over the ground, established churches at Snow Hill and Rehobeth, Maryland, and then went cross-country for God. He roved the country from the Carolinas to Boston, planting a church wherever he could, leaving behind him a good word for his faith and his Church wherever church-building proved impossible. He met welcome and woe; he was jailed in New York as a "strolling preacher" and brought to trial. He made such an eloquent plea for religious liberty that he was let off with a fine . . . and an acquittal! Which was no mean accomplishment, in New York!

Early, Makemie saw the need of organization, of a united Presbyterian front. The flock was scattered the length of the coast; the ministers saw one another seldom, if at all. That would never do, if the Presbyterians were to hold their own. In 1701, the first step was taken to unify their forces and an informal Presbyterial Conference was held in Philadelphia to ordain Jedekiah Andrews. Four years later, in 1705, the first American Presbytery was formed in the same city. John Hampton, an Irishman, George McNish, a Scotchman, Andrews, Makemie, Nathaniel Taylor and Samuel Davies constituted the Presbytery, of which Makemie was probably Moderator. Makemie describes it as "a meeting of ministers for ministerial exercise to consult the most proper measures for advancing religion and propagating Christianity." It turned out to be the parent organization of the American Presbyterians.

For the next quarter-century they grew fast. Irish, Scotch and English poured into the country, bringing each their separate viewpoints and creeds. Loosely, they all held to the Westminster Confession. With the passing years, there came a determined agitation for a law or requirement by which they might judge those who wished to enter the Presbyterian ministry and with which to hold them to their time-honored Calvinistic covenant, once they were in. Hence, the "Adopting Act of 1729," in which they definitely stated that they would guard to the end "the faith once delivered to the saints . . . pure and uncorrupt . . ." and that while they would keep out all who could not agree "with all the essential and necessary articles of said Confession," they would nevertheless treat those who disagreed with them in doctrine "with the same friendship, kindness, and brotherly love, as if they had not differed from us in such sentiments."

The Scotch-Irish knew what they wanted. The Adopting Act may look like a shackle to us, in 1936, but they were not living in 1936. They had spilled their blood over the Westminster Confession; to deny the Confession would be to deny everything they had fought for, bled for, died for; to defend it seemed their paramount duty. It meant to them what rain means to a farmer, the difference between life and death. So they insisted upon it. It caused dissension, division, trouble, later on, but they clung to it. "Grant, Lord," prayed one of their old elders, "that I may be right, for thou knowest I am hard to turn."

There they stood, at the crossroads of their American adventure. They had their Act as a measuring rod to judge their preachers and to guarantee their preaching;

they had their first administrative organization, the Philadelphia Presbytery. As time rolled on and the Presbytery became a Synod, we have a good cross-section of what the Presbyterian Church was and was to be in America. It was inclusive, sheltering English, Scotch, Irish and Welsh types; it was broad, generous, tolerant and insistent, so far as its own churches were concerned, upon its Calvinistic principles and its Covenanter heritage. These dead fathers of theirs should not have died in vain, they vowed; this faith purchased at so great a price should not evaporate; this God should not be lost.

Did they sing new hymns now, with their old Psalms? Did they sing "A charge to keep I have, a God to glorify . . ."?

Chapter VIII

THE PRESBYTERIANS

(II)

Man must have his creeds, his Adopting Acts; they are as necessary to satisfy the hunger of his mind and soul as bread is necessary to satisfy the hunger of his mortal frame. The early Presbyterians knew that. Even yet, more than most of us, they are creed-conscious. They got that from John Calvin, who started them thinking, and from the Covenanter, who encouraged them to write their thoughts in blood. They also learned from Calvin and the Scotch that a church with nothing more than a creed is like a ship without a sail, or a boiler without steam. A faith, to live, most have disciples, prophets, teachers, men on crosses, men ablaze. William Tennent was the living fire beneath the Presbyterian "boiler" in the Colonies. He was Irish.

He came here in 1718 with four sons (all ministers) and a lively, flashing style of revivalistic preaching and a firmly fixed idea that the only good preachers were educated preachers. (That was good Calvinism and good Presbyterianism; creeds and colleges have been the chief stock in trade of the men of the Geneva gown for more than four hundred years.)   There would be an educated ministry in America, swore Irish William Tennent, if he had to see to it himself.   He saw to it, himself.   He began with his own four sons, in the manse at Neshaminy, Pennsylvania; inasmuch as he had no campus and no faculty besides himself, he called it his "Log College."   What he lacked in equipment he made up in zeal; he had something to teach and he knew how to teach it and before the first semester was over, Log College had a reputation.   From a family affair it grew to be a national institution.   More boys sat down with the four brothers to hear him tell of Calvin and Knox, boys who eventually became the leading Presbyterian clerics of the country. To him and his Log College, says church-historian Webster, above all others, were due "the prosperity and enlargement of the Presbyterian Church."   Out of Neshaminy, in time, came fifty colleges and universities; out of it came the College of New Jersey, later known as Princeton, with a Nassau Hall named in honor of Dutch Reformed William of Orange and flying his royal Dutch banner of orange and black.

When death tapped the old teacher on the shoulder, his sons carried on.   Flesh of his flesh and spirit of his spirit, they preserved in their preaching the revivalistic fire and the high regard for education of their famous sire.   And like him, they came in the fullness of time.

Be it chance or be it God, that has always happened:
great men are forever on hand to meet great crises.
Washington was born for the Revolution, Luther for
the Reformation, the Tennant brothers for the Great
Awakening. In company with Frelinghuysen of the
Dutch Reformed, Jonathan Edwards the Congregationalist and Whitefield the Englishman, they preached the
glad tidings when the glad tidings most needed to be
preached. Whitefield, who was the free-lance, roving
prophet of the Awakening, liked them; he was especially
fond of brilliant young Gilbert Tennent, who preached
hell-fire and sin and redemption like a man of his own
heart. Young Tennent believed with all his heart that
the steam of revivalism was vital to the life of American
Presbyterianism, as a counterbalance to the cold tomes
of the Calvinistic creedalists; some of the older Presbyterian "engineers" thought otherwise; they clashed.
Pleading for greater care in the examination of preacher
candidates and for a greater reverence for the ancient
principles of the faith as taught at Log College and fear-
ing that his father's work was being discredited, Tennent
accused his Synod of laxity in godliness. Synod resented
that. Preachers took sides; those of the "Old Side" stood
against Tennent's revivalism, against the "roving evangelists" who entered the parishes of regularly appointed
ministers and staged their fly-by-night revivals; the
"New Side" men stood for the right of any man to

preach God anywhere, at any time, in any way he chose. Never could these twain meet, they thought; in 1741, the Presbytery of New Brunswick, which included Gilbert Tennent and most of New Jersey, was read out of the Synod. New Brunswick joined the Presbytery of New York, to form the Synod of New York. It was the first split in their ranks, a split which remained open and dangerous, like a great black scar across the face of the Church, for seventeen long years. Then cooler heads got at the problem, talked it over quietly and joined themselves into one Synod again, into the Synod of Philadelphia and New York. That's a habit the Presbyterians have; they have always managed, somehow, to bury the hatchet and to keep it buried.

In union there was strength; from the day of reunion to the hour when war broke out in 1775, there was a flash of missionary activity. John Eliot inspired them; John Eliot, who had been known as "the apostle to the Indians," who assembled his savages into praying villages and who left behind him the first American translation of the Bible and eleven thousand Christian Indians. David Brainerd was among the Indians in Pennsylvania and New Jersey in 1743; a full generation before the era of organized home missions, Geneva-gowned missionaries were to be found in the Ohio wilderness beyond Fort Pitt and among the Oneidas in New York; they were halted only by the impossible combination of Indian warfare,

French intrigue and the booming of the opening guns of the Revolution. Samuel Davies went down to Virginia and James Campbell rode in the Carolinas; James Hall worked seven months and thirteen days and was paid eighty-six dollars; John Lindley labored for four months and preached ninety-six times and received twelve dollars and fifty cents, payment in full, to date! Two years before Lexington, the Presbyterians were raising funds to send two Negro students from Princeton to Africa; in 1777, Samuel Doak was walking through Maryland and Virginia, driving before him an old flea-bitten mare loaded down with books. The books became a college—Washington College, at Salem, Tennessee, the first college west of the Alleghenies. By that time the Revolution was on and the soldiers of Christ were forced to drop the work of God in the wilderness to do the work of hell in war.

Long before Doak and Lexington, the Presbyterians had been getting ready for the Revolution. Bancroft says, "The first voice publicly raised in America to dissolve all connections with Great Britain came not from the Puritans of New England nor the Dutch of New York nor the planters of Virginia, but from the Scotch-Irish Presbyterians." That's right. In January of 1775, certain Scotch-Irish in council at Abingdon, Virginia, declared to all concerned that they could never submit their liberties or property to a venal British parliament or corrupt ministry. Most of the Presbyterians north and south were of the same sentiments about the Revolution; the Scotch-Irish nature was tinder made to order for the flames of war. Many an Englishman overseas, listening to them, called it the Presbyterian Rebellion, instead of the American Revolution; Horace Walpole informed Parliament that "Cousin America" had "run off with a Presbyterian parson."

They went at it as if their lives depended on it, with all the consecrated abandon of the old Covenanters, for whose ideal of freedom, they felt, they were once more at war and with the old enemy. The leading generals on Washington's staff were Presbyterians: Knox, Sullivan, Stark, Clinton, Montgomery (who died at Quebec), Mad Anthony Wayne, Morgan and Pickens; a good proportion of those who remained loyal through the hard days of the strife were Presbyterians; the log cabins of Valley Forge were full of them. General Washington was so impressed with them that he once said he would rally his Scotch-Irish troopers, if the war were lost and he had but one banner left, and plant a new republic on top of the Blue Ridge mountains, in spite of British, deserters, or whatnot. The Blue Ridge would have been a good spot for that; all through the South, during the Revolution, the battle cry was "No bishop, and no king!"

They were so loyal, perhaps, because their Presbyterian parsons whipped them on. Only two Presbyterian ministers went British and they were quickly cast into outer darkness. The rest were patriots of the patriots. There was John Witherspoon, for instance, president of the College of New Jersey; Scotch born, but with an American heart, he left the halls of learning for the political stump, where he did more than even Tom Paine or Patrick Henry or Paul Revere to tell the country that the British were coming; he talked, he wrote; wherever he went regiments sprouted from the ground. He served in the Continental Congress and he was the only Colonial clergyman to sign his name to the Declaration of Independence. (A document, by the way, in the handwriting of a Scotchman, Charles Thompson, the Secretary of Congress; printed by a Scotch-Irishman, Thomas Dunlop, and first read to the people by Captain John Nixon, also Scotch-Irish!) Witherspoon remains one of the great names of the period, one of the most talented and able ministers of all time in America and the perfect illustration of the militant Calvinist who, says one biographer, might be found almost anytime with "one knee bent before God and the other on the neck of a king."

They suffered and they won; they found that suffering, when triumphant, pays high wages. They came out of the Revolution in a most commanding position among the churches, quite the strongest of them all. Nearly two million out of the national population of three million were of Calvinistic stock and descent and that is a majority. Events played right into the hands of the majority: a Convention met in Philadelphia to adopt the national Constitution at the same hour that the Presbyterians met there to organize their first assembly. John Witherspoon was there, dividing his time between the politicians and the preachers. When the two bodies had adjourned, they had done pretty much the same thing. In their structure, in their series of courts and governing bodies and underlying principles, the Presbyterian Church and the American Government run almost parallel, are almost two peas in the same pod. Built side by side, at the same hour and by the same men, the two institutions may as well have been founded beneath the same roof.

Into the national Constitution went declarations to the effect that there was to be absolute religious and political freedom and equality in this new nation; into the records of the Presbyterian meeting went the famous "Declaration of 1788," which adopted the Westminster Confession of Faith as the creed of the Church and which said to the world: "There are truths and forms, with respect to which men of good characters and principles may differ. And in these they think it the duty, both of private Christians and societies, to exercise mutual forebearance toward each other." Two conventions, with a single thought; two groups of men, with the same

idea! That may have been one of the developments
which led Ranke, the great German historian, to say that
"John Calvin is the practical founder of America."

In the year 1800, the President of the United States
warned his people against the current "dissemination of
principles subversive to the foundation of all religious,
moral and social obligations . . ." that were abroad in the
land. The Presbyterians agreed with the President; they
were living, they said, in a day of total depravity. It
was fashionable to be irreligious and old-fashioned to
believe in God. Race-track bookies and saloonkeepers
grew richer while the churches grew poorer. Man, according to Jean Jacques Rousseau, was a "noble savage,"
sometimes more savage than noble, somewhat repulsive
in the war-paint of his self-sufficient egotism and bowing
low at the altars of a new religion which he called Na-
tionalism. It seemed to make little difference what a
man believed, or if he believed anything at all. "I am a
sect by myself," said Thomas Jefferson. That was the
trouble; there were too many sects. "Onward, Christian Soldiers, All one body we?" No, that was gone;
now it was "Every man for himself," with the devil
taking more than the hindmost. The Presbyterians were
worried about it. So worried that they did something
about it.

For years their strength had been in the old settlements, in the established towns; there they stood like the

Greeks at Thermopylæ against the onslaughts of the ma-
terialists and the agnostics and the atheists of the day;
there they began to realize that, if they were to win for
God, they must leave the settlements and range the
frontier, where the enemy, thanks to the primitive
forces of life out there, had his greatest strength. They
moved deliberately, carefully. Like an iceberg, or a
land-going glacier. "An intellectual glacier," a writer of
the period calls them, "an overwhelming mass of cold
dogma." Calvinistic dogma. It's unpopular now; it
was a lifesaver then. It was the antidote to the poison
of arrogant unbelief in the foundation principles of the
nation and the Church, and great would have been the
confusion and long delayed the march of American progress had the "glacier" not appeared. You can't just
knock those faith foundations from under a man and
leave him nothing but unbelief to stand on; you can't
blast out the foundations of a new nation and expect the
nation to endure. Dogma or no dogma, it was quite
what we needed in 1800.

As part of their campaign, the Presbyterians tried
something new. (That is a Presbyterian mannerism;
they have always been ready to experiment and they
have always shown the good sense and courage to drop
the experiment when they have found it wouldn't work.)
They tried a Plan of Union with the Congregationalists,
whereby the churches of the two groups moved together,

as one, into the missionary territory of the new West. It worked for a while and then it collapsed, partly because there came a laxness of discipline and polity when the two institutions were merged, partly because of a disagreement over missionary methods and partly because the Presbyterians felt that their moneys were being diverted to build Congregational Churches and because certain "novelties of New England theology" were creeping in. Debates came up in presbyteries and assemblies, between New School men and Old School and in 1837 the blow fell; the Old School men came to power, abrogated the Plan of Union, expelled four New School Synods and split the Church in twain.

No, into three parts. Back in 1810, the Cumberland Presbytery had withdrawn from the Church to form one of their own. The disagreement was over the educational requirements of the ministry; caught in the wave of revivalism which swept the South, the Cumberland men insisted that they must have preachers and have them quickly, to care for the new flocks scattered over the mountains and country districts of the Cumberland; must have them, whether they had much education or none. There was no time to waste on school, they said; they needed men strong in the Spirit to hold their scattered forts. When Synod disagreed, the dissenters set up the Cumberland Presbyterian Church. Fifty years later they had one hundred thousand members.

Thus were they divided on the eve of the Civil War into New School, Old School and Cumberland branches. Schism was a cancer, destroying from within.

But all was not schism; there were builders in these days, as well as dividers. Steeples were going up in the forests where tepees had been before; trading-post log cabins, with the curses of the trappers lingering in their beams, gave themselves up to the sighing of sinners and the shouts of the saved in Presbyterian prayer meetings. The black Geneva gown of the Calvinist followed in the wake of Lewis and Clark and the coonskin cap, to do for God what the explorers had done for the government. They preached; they stood on upturned nail kegs in village stores and told of the mercies of God; they turned taverns into tabernacles and barrooms into sanctuaries; they froze in the forest and they died of thirst in the desert and strong young men stepped over their graves to build another church, farther West. They built meetinghouses and they built schools. Creeds and colleges! From 1812 to 1836, when shrewd observers thought the Presbyterian Church was breaking up, they built the greatest of their theological seminaries: Princeton, Auburn, Allegheny, Columbia, Lane, McCormack, Union in Virginia and Union in New York. They created a Home Missionary Society and an Educational Society and they tried another experiment, with parochial schools. The experiment failed and they dropped it. Breaking up? Not they. Churches with such temperament and energy can *never* break up.

Facing west, they were conscious of a storm approaching at their backs, a storm gathering strength in the south, sweeping north and east and threatening the work of the Church and the life of the nation. The Presbyterians were as alive to its coming as they had been alive to the coming of the Revolution; in 1787, the Synod of New York and Pennsylvania had advocated education and emancipation for the Negro; the Synod of Ohio went on record in 1815 as opposing barter in slaves; the Assembly of 1818 had something to say of slavery as "inconsistent with the law of God." Try as they would, they could not get rid of the issue; slavery was a Banquo's ghost, forever coming back to upset the love feasts of the Church. By 1837, a split was in evidence; by 1857, several Southern Synods had broken away to form the United Synod of the Presbyterian Church. When war came in the spring of '61, forty-seven presbyteries of the Old School persuasion formed a Presbyterian Church in the Confederate States of America. In 1864, these two bodies merged and called themselves the Presbyterian Church in the United States, and such they are today. Popularly, we call it the Southern Presbyterian Church.

It is easy for us, three-quarters of a century later, to deplore all this, to point the finger of shame at the tragic divisions of the war; easy, for we are quite removed from the furor of the hour. Judging from our behavior in crises and conflicts since then, we should probably have done exactly as they did. Enough to say here that there were sincere and Christian men on both sides of this slavery issue; that there were truth and justice to be found on either side; be it enough, too, to say that the *whole* truth about the Civil War has not yet been written in novel or textbook; we are still too close to it. But whatever chagrin we may feel over the division of the Church should be lost when we consider the manner in which the Church has unified her forces since the battle flags of the Rebellion were furled. That wiseacre who stands on the street corner asking, "Why don't the Protestants all get together?" has something to learn when he looks the facts in the face. Protestants *have* been getting together and the Presbyterians have been showing the way. Proceeding on the assumption that it would be more Christian to unify their own house first, before making gestures of reunion with other denominations, they have kept steadily at it; in 1870, Old School and New School branches were reunited on the basis of the old Westminster Confession, to be joined in 1906 by the Cumberland branch and in 1920 by the Welsh Calvinistic Methodists. Together, these make up the Presbyterian Church in the United States of America, the largest group of Presbyterians in the country. Today there are but nine different bodies of American Presbyterians, with nearly three million members. Over two millions of these are found in the two main groups, in the Presbyterian Church in the United States of America (the northern division) and in the Presbyterian Church in the United States (the southern group). Five of the remaining seven groups have come to us directly from Scotland or England; all of them are seriously considering consolidation and reunion. Add to this strictly American movement the mergers of Presbyterians in Canada and Scotland; add to it the recent "conversations" with American Congregationalists and Methodists on the subject of organic union; add to it the grouping of Calvinistic churches here and abroad into an "Alliance of Reformed Churches Throughout the World Holding the Presbyterian System;" add to it the establishment of a permanent Department of Church Union in the Presbyterian Church in the United States of America and it would appear that the gentleman on the street corner has something to learn about "getting together."

Relentlessly, the Presbyterian glacier crawled on toward the edge of civilization; relentlessly, it moved upon the old frontier. The Presbyterians moved into the undeveloped West, settled it, developed it, Christianized it; they drove a phalanx into the ranks of the undeveloped Negro, helping to educate and orient him and to save his soul; they moved on, in time, to undeveloped Alaska,

Labrador, Porto Rico.   Schools for the colored shot up
in the South; a hospital went up at Point Barrow, Alaska,
the farthest north white settlement on the road to the
Pole, farther north than brave little Doctor Grenfell
ever paddled his canoe; Doctor Griest holds forth there,
preaching with scalpel and lancet, breaking into the
headlines when Lindbergh comes his way, when Will
Rogers and Wiley Post meet death in the frozen Arctic.
From Nome to Mexico and in sixteen foreign countries,
you will find men and women in Genevan black.

But the frontier after the Civil War was not so much
physical as moral, social, intellectual, economic.   A new
world was here, a different world.   The astronomers had
pushed back the boundaries of the universe; archeolo-
gists were digging out old civilizations and architects
were creating new skylines.   A new psychology, a new
learning, a new morality, a new society had been born.
Jay Gould and "Jim" Fiske and "Uncle Daniel" Drew
and John D. Rockefeller and canny Andrew Carnegie
ushered in a new era of business and Bill Tweed introduced us to a new politics.   The rich got richer and the
poor got poorer, millionaires doubled and paupers tripled,
a few waxed rich and thousands cried for bread.   A tidal
wave of immigration rose in Europe and crashed down
on Ellis Island, filling our cities with seething, unas-
similated thousands of foreign-born, the pockets of the
industrialists with unexpected gold and the hearts of

churchmen and social workers with frank despair. In the midst of this world of hocus-pocus transformation stood the Church of Christ, preaching the gospel of the son of an obscure carpenter in Nazareth, nineteen hundred years old. Could Christ last, in all this? Could the two, the old Gospel and the New World, be joined? Could Nazareth and Calvary compete with Wall Street and Ellis Island?

Well, judge for yourself. A civilization has collapsed, since the Civil War, in a World War; yet the population of the Church of Christ has been growing faster than the population of the world and that Church is saying, as never before, that such a collapse shall never come again. Ellis Island has passed the peak of its labors and millions of foreigners are now American and you will find their churches scattered from the Battery to the Golden Gate. Wall Street has fallen and is struggling to rise again, the stock market has become a crazy thermometer, industries and businesses have gone down and out, yet the Church is still about the Father's business, stronger than ever. Psychologies have come and gone, little learnings have had their day, skylines have leaped toward the sky and crumbled into dust, yet the good news of Christ still holds the headlines of the press and the hearts of men and the still small voice is heard above the din of the traffic of the marketplace. Why? How did *that* happen?

It happened because the Church played fair with God and man, with the everlasting truth and the shifting hour. It happened because the Presbyterians, for one, kept their covenant with the dead and their vision of the living. The Presbyterian now staged two drives, sought two objectives: he would protect and defend and conserve the permanent values of his faith and he would meet the moods and methods of the New World with new moods and methods of his own.

First, he protected his heritage. As the new century dawned, there came a more and more insistent demand for a revision of the Westminster Confession of Faith; that Confession, the Presbyterians felt, no longer adequately expressed their deepest convictions; they were children of the nineteenth and twentieth centuries and not of the seventeenth. That Confession could be made, must be made, as usable and pertinent to their day as it had been to their fathers'. They did it. Did it by the sane method of evolution, instead of the destructive method of revolution. There's a lesson in that: it is far better to go slow and err seldom than to go fast and crash. Stabilization in progress is not only good but necessary; more genuine benefit has come to Church and State and society from the careful Calvinists than from all the thousand and one useless religious sects that have flattered themselves that they were revolutionary and therefore good! The Presbyterians modified, revised, adjusted their creed, losing none of it that was vital, yet making room within it for all manner of man and mind. There were revisions from 1889 to 1923, in which year there came an "Affirmation Designated to Safeguard the Unity and Liberty of the Presbyterian Church," which called them back to the spirit of 1729 and the Declaration of 1788 and to the good old principle on which they had been founded, the principle of the freedom of the individual conscience. The Affirmation stated clearly their allegiance to their own faith and their tolerance of others. That is a good position. A Christian position.

That cost something. It cost, some say, too much. In the heat of argument between men of the old order and the new, names were hurled: "Modernist!" "Fundamentalist!" "Affirmationist!" "Middle-of-the-Roader!" Heresy trials were inevitable. There were the trials of Doctor Swing in 1874, of Professors Briggs and Preserved Smith in 1901, the Fosdick case in 1924 and the Machen case in 1935. To the unchurched, all this was disgraceful; to those within the pale, it was regrettable. But it all served a purpose; theological debate is as justifiable in the councils of the Church as political debate is in the Congress of the United States. It educates, it clears the air, it produces in time a peace of understanding which could come in no other way. Men argue most over things that matter most. And religion matters.

Meanwhile, the other drive was on, the drive to square

the Gospel against the problems of the world. This was the age in which the Church discovered humanity and the social teachings of Jesus and we find the preachers insisting in a new earnestness that Jesus Christ be followed and obeyed in the office and mill and shop as well as in the pew. Did the economic system permit thirty-five per cent of the population to hold ninety-five per cent of the wealth? Then the economic system was wrong, unchristian, and it should be changed. Were children snatched from the schoolroom and a decent chance at life to labor and die in the sweatshop or the cotton mill? Then the preachers would fight child labor in the name of Jesus Christ. Was labor victimized by the employer-profiteer? Then the Church would fight for labor. Did industry reap a harvest of profit at the expense of human life? Then industry must be Christianized. Did men still deny Christ for Mars and go to war? Then away with war! This was the new frontier. Religion, said the preachers, was a seven-day affair. Christ was either master of the whole of life, or master of none of it.

Early in 1905, the Presbyterians created a Department of Church and Labor, that they might do their part intelligently. In 1910 a prophet of the new order, Doctor Charles Stelzle, had the Presbyterian Board of Home Missions buy an old abandoned church on Fourteenth Street, New York, a neighborhood predominantly foreign. He put in some furniture, swept out the cobwebs and named it Labor Temple. It was to live up to its name, he said, to be a sanctuary and a forum for the worker. Of course, there was opposition; he had to import Theodore Roosevelt to say it was all right before he could open it at all. But he opened it. It is there today, the outward physical expression of an inner, spiritual vision, a forum, a clearinghouse of truth where Communists and Christians sit down together to talk of labor and love, where Christ is preached and the labor unions have offices. It is a sign, a symbol, an experiment, an evidence of the Presbyterian effort to face up to the new day.

The 1934 Assembly declared boldly that "Christians cannot give their support to war. . . . Men must have some active part in the control of industry to which their lives are given. . . . There ought to be a universal system of unemployment insurance. . . . New motives besides those of money-making and self-interest must be developed in order that they may have an economic system more consistent with Christian ideals. . . ."

And here is Doctor John McDowell, Moderator, preaching his retiring sermon at the same Assembly: "A saved soul in a saved body, living in a saved community, is not only the best credential for Christianity; it is the only credential that satisfies the demands of New Testament Christianity and meets the need of the world."

Here speaks the Presbyterian Church in America; here is her philosophy, her ideal, her plan. Champion of the timeless Christ and of the human underdog, lover of liberty and builder of governments, enthusiast in education and evangelism and cleanser of society, she has been an inestimable force for righteousness in the past; she is a power for progress today and an anchor against the storms in the days that are yet to be.

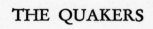

THE QUAKERS

CHAPTER IX

THE QUAKERS

On a hill above Lichfield, a man in leather breeches took off his shoes. He walked a mile into the town, moved slowly up and down the streets and across the crowded marketplace shouting, "Woe to bloody Lichfield!" No man tried to stop him, no one put a hand upon him. As eerily as a messenger from another world, as darkly ominous as Amos on the Tekoa road, he went on and back up his hill again, still crying "Woe!" The year was 1651. The man, George Fox. The place, England. The English said he was peculiar, a religious ranter, a disturber of the British peace and mayhap a lunatic. Fox said the Lord had sent him; he took the Lord's sending seriously and did what the Lord commanded him to do. He went all over England shouting "Woe!"

Measured by Lichfield in 1651, George Fox *was* peculiar. He laughed at the law and he slapped conventionality in the face. He refused to take off his hat to anyone, to judge, mayor, bishop, even King. He said there was nothing in the Bible about that; hat-lifting was a recent French importation. Were not all men

equal? Who was a king, anyway, but a costumed com-
moner? True courtesy lay in the heart, not on the head.
He refused to take an oath in court; Matthew says,
"Swear not at all," and that was that. Court oaths were
ridiculous; a Christian *always* told the truth. The Bible
also said, "Thou shalt not kill." That meant killing in
war, as well as private murder. Fox hated war and he
would have nothing to do with it. It was unchristian.
Down with it! And down with slavery. No man had
any right to enslave another; God had made us all of one
free blood. England should strike the chains from her
African slaves; England should be more merciful with
the felons she had chained up in filthy, lousy dungeons.
Her prison system was all wrong, barbarous, wicked.
George Fox, ranter, was the only seventeenth-century
religious leader to decry the awful penology of England.

Fox loathed the careless churches of his day and the
careless preachers in them. Not that he wanted to
destroy them; he only wanted to purify them. He called
them "steeple houses," their preachers, "priests," Midas-
minded hirelings, working for pay, demanding gold for
handing out the bread of life. Men, he held, were not
saved by pious sermon and sacrament, but by direct
communion with God. There was a direct illumination
from God in the heart, an illumination he called the
Inner Light, a firsthand contact or experience with the
Divine. Men should shun rituals and preachers' sermons,

Fox said, and sit quietly and wait in the hushed hour for God to touch off the faith candle in the heart. It was a personal business and it required the services of no church, no priest. He abhorred theology; he called all doctrines "notions," he insisted on experience. God speaks. Be still, man, and listen!

What could happen to such a man, in such an England, where religion was established and where religious custom was sacrosanct? Well, what happened to Jesus, when he opposed the established faith of Jerusalem? To Peter, Paul, Huss, Savonarola, Wyclif? Fox was punished for breaking out of line, for thinking ahead of his fellows. He was cursed, mobbed, stoned, clubbed, locked in dank lousy dungeons with rats and lice and death and God. What fools they were, those enemies of his, trying to club his idea to death, thinking they could crush out the brave truth he had beneath their red and rowdy heathen heels. They did more to spread his faith than any word he ever spoke. When they tried to lock him in, they let out his secret. When they clubbed him, they advertised him. When they tried to shout him down, their shouting was a sounding board for his quiet explanation: "I have heard a Voice!"

They came to him in jail and offered to make him an officer in Cromwell's army if he would stop his foolish talk of brotherhood and peace, his mad opposition to the use of arms. He could have epaulets, position, a horse;

he could give commands, he could be a captain and a gentleman. He stood there in his filthy cell, his clothes unspeakable, with the vermin crawling over him, and he laughed at them. He despised their epaulets, their uniforms. "Now I see," said Oliver Cromwell, "there is a people risen and come up that I cannot win either with gifts, honors, offices, or places. . . ." Fox was serious about his Light.

So were his followers. Whoever went with him suffered and liked it. They were sentenced by judges who dropped their eyes in shame as they passed judgment; they converted their jailers; they were begged by sheriffs and mayors please, please to get out of town and please, please to stay out. They came back to town. Mobs tore them from their street pulpits and beat them near to death; established preachers hounded them; false witnesses lied about them, solemnly, on oath, in court; England was afraid of them. They were so terribly calm, so devastatingly meek. In their hearts was the peace of which Matthew Arnold wrote:

> "Calm soul of all things! be it mine
> To feel amid the city's jar,
> That there abides a peace of thine
> Man did not make and cannot mar!"

They had something deep within them that baffled England could not reach, nor understand.

The tree of persecution bore its certain fruit; England, finally, gave up in all her might and majesty and established dignity to this handful of the meek who had turned the other cheek. In 1654, with persecution going strong, they were a despised minority; in 1659, they numbered thousands and they were a threat.

Names came. At first they called themselves the "Children of the Light." Then, "Friends." One day George Fox stood before a jesting judge and told him the time had come for even judges to "quake and tremble before the Lord." "Ah," said the jester, "so you are Quakers, are you?" It did not fit them; needles in haystacks are easier to find than cowards among the Friends. But it stuck. Officially, to cold history, they are the Society of Friends; to this admiring world, since the day of the jesting magistrate, they have been the Quakers.

Lest England forget the Quaker when she stopped hounding him, the Quaker said to all concerned, toward the end of the Restoration period: "We utterly deny all outward wars and strife, and fightings with outward weapons, for any end, or under any pretense whatever; this is our testimony to the whole world." Remember that. It means something. It is as important as the Inner Light.

Missionary adventurers went out. To the Continent, to Ireland, to the West Indies. The island of Barbados teemed with them, shook under their preaching against war and slavery. (There were ten thousand slaves on this island, out of twenty-five thousand inhabitants.) Some of the adventurers moved on, to New England.

Now Anne Hutchinson had been preparing the soil for them in New England; Dame Anne was Quaker in everything but name. Being that, she was bundled off to Rhode Island. When she walked stiff and straight from Pastor Wilson's church in Boston after being given over to Roger Williams and the devil, a little lady rose from her pew and joined her in the aisle. The little lady was Mary Dyer, some day to become a Quaker, some day to strangle to death in a hangman's noose on Boston Common.

Mary and Anne were not out of sight when another Mary and Anne arrived to pester the Puritan: Mary Fisher and Anne Austin came from Barbados in the good ship *Swallow*, stepped from the deck into the town jail. They were charged only with being Quakers; they were stripped, searched for signs of witchcraft, denied light and air and ink and shipped away when the *Swallow* weighed anchor. The jailer confiscated their bedding and their Bibles; Massachusetts breathed easier. "Why was it," asked George Bishop of the magistrates, "that the coming of two women so shook ye, as if a formidable army had invaded your borders?" Two days after Mary and Anne sailed out of the harbor, eight new Quakers sailed in.

The eight were jailed, examined, shipped away. More ships arrived. More Quakers. It was a tide, a torrent. Seventy-five of them stood in court in Sandwich in 1658, with their hats on; men were flogged and branded and banished and women were whipped. Envenomed laws cropped their ears, drove hot irons through their tongues, tied them to cart tails and whipped them across the state and into fame. At last Massachusetts tried hanging. Massachusetts hung three men and Mary Dyer. As her dead body swung and twisted in the wind, Master Humphrey Atherton bethought himself of a joke: "She hangs there like a flag," he said. Aye, a flag. An humble nonresister's flag that won against the ear-cropper and the executioner, against bigotry and narrowness and superstition and savagery. The flag of the Quaker! The flag of conscience, justice, freedom, glory, God!

Why? Why all this? Why were they hated so, so cut and bled and slaughtered? There are reasons. Sometimes the Quakers went too far. There were fanatics among them who were violent, contentious, disorderly, silly; who did things and said things for which, should they do or say them today, they would certainly be clapped into the nearest, strongest jail. But the Puritan objection went deeper than this. While he agreed with the Quaker in loving righteousness and hating tyranny, he stood opposed to him in all else. The

Quakers were individualists; the Puritans were a Judaistic clan. The Quaker kept his hat on in the presence of the King; to the Puritan, State was as holy as Church, one with it, inseparable, inviolate, a mark for laud and honor. The Quaker taught tolerance; that, to the Puritan, was a devil's doctrine and a thrust at the heart of his politico-religious, theocratic commonwealth. They had next to nothing in common; they could no more live in love together than arrogant Nero could have lived in love with Jesus Christ. When they met, blood flowed. And in their century blood was cheap.

It stopped when the people became sickened of it and when King Charles II commanded them to stop it. A Quaker brought that word from Charles; he stood before old Endicott with his hat on and Endicott dared not make him take it off. The grisly day was done. So was Endicott's theocracy. The Quakers were turned loose and forgotten. They had won their fight. The meek had inherited Massachusetts.

Nowhere else in the colonies did they suffer so. There were persecutions in the South and in the Middle States, but they were short-lived. Rhode Island, from the first, received them with open arms and elected them to public office for more than a century. New York opposed them for a brief period under Stuyvesant. New Jersey, first of the real Quaker strongholds, had three Quaker governors and Speaker Samuel Jenings of the Assembly.

And Jersey had John Woolman. "Get the writings of
John Woolman by heart," says Charles Lamb. For the
writings of John Woolman are the plain account of a
colonial saint talking, thinking, acting with his God. He
loved men, sincerely. All men. White men. Red men.
Negroes. Eventually, he loved Negroes most. Eventually, the drives of his life simmered down to one: he
wanted to free the Negro slave. He was impatient with
delay about that; do it now, now, now. More than any
other Quaker, he aroused the conscience of the Friends
against slavery; more than any other man that ever lived,
he forced the world to be rid of it. With Whittier, he
was the flower of American Quakerism.

A great Quaker migration moved southward from
1725 to 1775, into Virginia and the Carolinas. They
preached against slavery in slavery's stronghold; they
said it was sinful to sell rum to an Indian; they refused
to take oaths and they would not bear arms and they
stood before Lord Baltimore with their hats on. They
produced John Archdale, peer of Colonial governors,
Governor of three great states, who practiced a new
charity with the poor and a new tolerance with the
Spanish Catholics in Florida, who built good roads and
good government with Christ as the head of the corner.

Meanwhile, an Admiral who hated Quakers died and
gave the Quakers their big chance. The Crown owed
the Admiral sixteen thousand pounds; the Crown offered

to pay off in land. In cheap, wild American land, **to** the Admiral's heir. So it happened that Quaker William Penn, son of Quaker-hater Admiral Penn, received by royal grant that great tract of forest lying "north of Maryland and on the east bounded by the Delaware River." Just for good measure, the Duke of York threw in what is now the State of Delaware. Penn wanted to call it Sylvania (woodland). The King wrote the old Admiral's name in front of that. Pennsylvania. The "Holy Experiment." A scheme that only a Quaker could think of.

There was no military force in Quaker Pennsylvania; love ruled in place of blunderbuss. Conscience was wholly free in religion, politics, State, Church. All were equal. The government was democratic to the nth degree; the people ruled. There was a Charter from the King, a Constitution from the people. "Friends," said Penn, "if in the constitution by charter there be anything that jars, alter it!" Sang a great poet:

"Here the free spirit of mankind, at length,
    Throws its fetters off."

The world cheered. Settlers flocked in. Towns grew. A great city grew. They called it Philadelphia, the City of Brotherly Love.

Brotherhood slipped its last checkrein here; in the fall of 1682, Penn sat under an elm at Shackamaxon with the Indians and made "the only treaty never sworn to and never broken." It was a treaty involving a transfer of land and a new league of brotherhood; it was a gentlemen's agreement, between gentlemen red and gentlemen white. Neighboring colonists laughed at it, for neighboring colonists had another way of dealing with the Indian; they thought it better to sell him rum and cheat him of his land while he lay drunk; they lied to the Indian, insulted, outraged, robbed and murdered him. All that was taboo, in Pennsylvania. The Indian was a man, a friend, a brother. The Indian liked that. So for more than seventy years, while the wise and laughing neighboring colonist was massacred and driven from one ghastly Indian war to another, Pennsylvania lived in peace with the red man. True, Indian politics may have had as much to do with that as Quaker piety; the Algonquin, with whom Penn sat under the Shackamaxon elm, was tired and exhausted from war with other tribes. But even exhausted Indians, provided with rum and muskets and cheated of their land, have been known to take the warpath. They never took it in Pennsylvania; the Quaker experiment in Christian brotherhood paid good dividends; the Holy Experiment worked. The Indian had been greeted as a man and he turned out to be a man.

The Negro was a brother, too, though he was a slave. The Quaker never liked that bondage of black by white and said so plainly from the start. (They were not far, yet, from the man in leather breeches.) The German Friends in Germantown said in 1688 that ". . . to bring men hither or to sell or rob them against their will, we stand against." At first, they only stood against, tolerating, but condemning. Then they began to fight it, from the inside out. In 1758, thanks to John Woolman, the Philadelphia Friends refused to let "sit in meeting" any Quaker owning a slave; in 1776, slave owners were being expelled from the society; by the close of the eighteenth century there was no such thing as a Quaker slave, except where legal complications were involved. A man could own slaves if he chose to; but his fellow Quakers chose to disown him, if he so decided.

If God writes in a judgment book, as some believe, He has long since written this, "The Quaker was the first American to wake to the fact that the Negro was a man; a man with a soul. His sect was the first to rid itself of slavery, the first of the Christians to wipe away the stain." And man could write this in his book, "If all Colonies in 1760 had been Quaker Colonies, there could have been no Civil War in 1860."

The Quakers stepped down from power in Pennsylvania in 1756. Rather than pay a tax to support a war against the Delawares and Shawnees, they resigned from office and handed over the state they had founded. But their influence remained; it stalked, a godly ghost, across the Delaware and up the coast. In every colony Quakers refused to fight, to mistreat the Indian, to hold slaves or to manufacture, sell, or drink liquor. That's one reason why the Friends are a "small" sect; they meant business.

And there was another reason why they stayed small. They lost their vision, their world outlook. While they were persecuted, they were a power; when it stopped, their effectiveness stopped. They withdrew into themselves, became more and more a peculiar people, told off from others by peculiar habits of speech and dress. They became troubled by little things, little sins, little errors, while the larger errors of the world escaped them. They huddled over their Inner Light, denied it air and freedom and almost smothered it. While at first they had been pioneers in elementary education, they had always lacked real educational vision; they built no Harvards, no Princetons, no Yales to prepare their youth for the world aborning; they thought their Inner Light sufficient unto everything, forgetting that worship and faith are of the mind as well as of the soul. They lost their place, their chance. George Fox saw it coming: when he died in 1691, he prayed with his dying gasp, "Mind (the) poor Friends in America."

That went on until a crisis called the Revolution came. They believed in freedom and they hated tyranny. But they also hated war. Now, with the Colonies fighting for freedom against tyranny, the Quaker must choose sides. He chose quietly, with full knowledge aforethought of what it would cost him. Before the war was on, he had decided. While Boston was throwing a cargo of tea into the Bay, two Philadelphia tea merchants, receiving a cargo at the same time, paid the captain for his unwelcome freight and told him to take it back to England. And when New York demanded of them a roll of all Quakers from sixteen to sixty, they replied, "We are of the mind we cannot comply!" They could not, as a body, join the war. War was unchristian. They were Christians, or trying to be. That was all. They wanted freedom, but not at such a price. A handful broke away and joined the army; they were the "Free" or "Fighting" Quakers, and Betsy Ross, who stitched a flag for General Washington, was one of them. A ridiculous half-dozen went British. But by and large, they refused to have anything to do with the war, to fight it or support it or to help either party to it.

They were plundered as ingrates by the Continentals, as fools by the British. Their meetinghouses were destroyed, their homes were burned and their farms were ruined; their property was seized when they refused to pay war taxes; their school-teachers were imprisoned for refusing to take an oath of allegiance; twenty of them were banished to Winchester, Virginia, without the decency of a trial. *But the Quaker did not fight.* He

preached peace and he stood by his preaching. He put
out of his Society anyone who went to the fighting. He
put out Thomas Mifflin, later governor of Pennsylvania;
he put out General Nathanael Greene. "Have your war
if you want it," they said in effect. "But expect no
help from us. Not one cent. Not one man. You
choose Mars. We choose Christ. So be it."

John Dickinson is typical. John Dickinson was an
able statesman, signing every great state paper leading up
to the Revolution. He wrote appeals to King and English people, he signed the Declaration of Rights and the
Articles of Confederation, but he refused to sign the
Declaration of Independence. That was premature, he
said, unnecessary. There was a better way, the way of
statesmanship, arbitration, understanding. The country would not take his way? Very well, then. He
stepped aside and let the Revolution sweep past him.
John Dickinson loved his country, but he loved Christ
more. He was powerless to stop the bloody affair, but he
would not take part in it. "His life," writes Rufus
Jones, "is typical of Quaker influence, potent to the out-
break of war, suddenly and strikingly impotent after it
becomes a fact."

Yet man might well write again in his judgment book,
"If Parliament and the Continental Congress had been
packed with Quakers, there would have been no Revolutionary War."

A reformation was sweeping the Society while revolution swept the Colonies. Awake at last to the perils of introspection, they tried hard to correct the abuses of their wasted years; they became more active than ever against slavery and liquor; they began building schools and spreading Quaker literature. It was splendid. And it was late. Too late. It might have worked wonders for them had not the god of controversy thrown his sly wrenches in their church gears. This was the century of the Great Division, of three great divisions. Divisions, strange to say, over doctrine! Every church in Christendom should meditate on this: the most Christian church of all met its first catastrophic defeat when it fell to bitter charge and countercharge over the theology its founder despised! Some broke away from the old body in the midst of the New Light agitation early in the new century; the "great" division came in 1827-28, when Elias Hicks, brilliant, popular and liberal, led out (involuntarily!) a group who taught that Christ was a spiritual genius, the greatest of men, but human and liable to sin, and that the gospels were "a history more or less accurate." That was Hicks and Hicksism; it split American Quakerism cleanly into Orthodox and Hicksite Quakers. The Hicksites have been a powerful group; proceeding on the principle that there should be fullest liberty in matters of doctrine and giving special attention to matters of social reform; they have made no mean contribution. They have fought for peace and the slave and education; they built Swarthmore College; they had a fine school, for years, in Virginia, with at least one famous student in attendance, a boy named Robert E. Lee.

Two other splits made the rout complete, before the century was out. In 1840 John Wilbur led a rebellion; his chief bone of contention was the relative authority of the Scriptures and the spirit. His sympathizers were called Wilburites; they never attained importance numerically, for they could not keep their ranks intact from counter-rebellion. Out of their movement (plus a few recruits from the [Orthodox] Yearly Meeting of Philadelphia) came the "Primitive Quakers." These were smaller yet; in 1934 they reported a total membership of fifteen!

Subtle, unseen forces were pushing them together in these years, in spite of their arguments on doctrine; while some of them were debating with Hicks and Wilbur, others were working on a railroad. On a subtle, unseen railroad known to us as the Underground Railway, which was busy slipping slaves to freedom in the free states or in Canada. Above ground, the Quaker protest against slavery kept up a steady broadside of pamphlets and propaganda; a poet in Vermont wrote against it in letters of fire, with a pen far mightier than any sword. John Greenleaf Whittier told of

". . . God's own image bought and sold!
America to market driven,
And bartered as the brute for gold."

But Whittier, like the good Quaker he was, never wanted
war:

"We grasp the weapons He has given,—
The Light and Truth and Love of Heaven."

It was a moral warfare the Friends were waging; they
wanted war no more to free the slave than they had
wanted war to free the Colonies. But war came, as a
result of the long drip of their preaching and the fervor
of the abolitionist. When it came, the Quaker behaved
quite as he had behaved in the Revolution.

There was a bit more freedom of choice among them
than in 1776; many more, proportionately, took up the
weapons of Mars and marched with the contending
armies. A Quaker wrote, "We are coming, Father
Abraham"; the Fifteenth Pennsylvania Regiment had
so many Friends that it was dubbed "The Quaker
Regiment." But most of these, to be honest, were
Quaker only by right of birth and not by right of
inner conviction; they were nominal Friends, if they
were Friends at all. Most of them kept faith with the
man in leather breeches. There were penalties, tortur-
ings, persecutions, killings. In the South, where every
man was needed and where anti-slavery Quakerism had

been in bad standing for years, their suffering was acute. They were hung up by the thumbs and deprived of food and drink and forced into humiliating poverty and want, but *they did not fight*. Indeed, they stood it so well that they made their persecutors ashamed of themselves. The wife of Seth Luflin received a letter from the officer who had tried to make her husband fight: "It is my painful duty to inform you that Seth W. Luflin died at Windsor Hospital on the eighteenth of December, 1864. He died, as he had lived, a true, humble and devoted Christian: true to his faith and religion. . . . We pitied, and sympathized with him." That letter says more than volumes could say of the triumph of the Quaker in the Civil War.

At the end of the war, the Quakers of North Carolina actually showed an increase in membership! And just to show that they intended to stand by their battle-scarred standards, they formed a national Peace Association of Friends in America. Peace, after all this!

At the end of the war, too, General Grant became President Grant. A heckled President Grant, whose friends betrayed him to make his administration a study in corruption and scandal. There was a railroad scandal, a liquor scandal. Jay Gould and Jim Fiske duped the hero of Appomattox and created a financial debacle; the men he had put in charge of the Indian work cheated the white man's government, now that the red man had nothing left for them to take. Grant was rather helpless at the hands of the financiers, but he knew how to handle the Indian situation. He knew the Quaker well, he knew of Penn at Shackamaxon, he knew the long and honorable record of the Society of Friends in their treatment of the American Indian. So he asked them to come in to help him, to help straighten out the tangle of administration in Indian affairs, to help him extend justice once more to the long-suffering "savage." He asked the very men who had refused to help him fight Lee to help him pacify the Indian and to train him in the arts of peace. The Quaker accepted and went to work. The Quaker succeeded, bringing peace and converting scores to Christianity. He converted sullen, vengeful Steamboat Frank, a murderous Modoc, made a preacher out of him, made a pacifist out of him. His murdering days were done when the Inner Light flared in him; he never fought again, for any cause or any man.

Peace gave impulse to the old humanitarian efforts of the Friends. Work for the Negroes grew apace; Southland College, in Arkansas, was one of the first reconstruction efforts. Work with underprivileged children had started as far back as 1849, when the Quaker "Association for Relief of Sick Children in the Summer Season" was founded; now the maintenance of summer camps became a passion, a science. There was increased zeal in work for the prisoner; Sarah Smith worked miracles in the Indiana penitentiary. The Quakers bore down more

heavily than ever against the liquor traffic; there were
more and more disownments for the manufacture, sale or
use of alcohol. "Thee" and "Thou" dropped almost out of
sight and Quakers walked in modern dress. Great colleges were fostered: Haverford, Bryn Mawr. They
gradually gave ground in the South, where their determination against slavery had outlawed them; they lost their
grip in New England. So they moved West, where there
were fresh harvests waiting and room for all. Their
wagon trains crawled across Indiana, Ohio, Kansas; they
sat in the quiet in California and Oregon, waiting for the
Voice to tell them where to go next. Then they went on to
build mission stations in Africa, China, Syria, Japan, in
the Far East and Far West, in India, Cuba, Alaska and
Mexico.

The end of the century discovered them still divided
into four groups, still united in their humanitarian efforts
for their fellow men. The division lines meant less and
less after 1900; the old tags were wearing out and falling off. They united in correcting abuses in the prisons
and the jails, inspiring the nation to reform the prisoner
and not to break him. They set up coffeehouses in
Philadelphia as a substitute for the saloon years before
the Prohibitionists realized that such a substitute was
necessary; they fought for the wage slaves, for the under-
dogs of labor before trade unions were more than a
dream. And when, in the early years of the twentieth

century, the machine had introduced a new industrial order and therefore a new social order, the Quaker stood like flint for a Christian attitude in the inevitable conflicts and disturbances which arose as we tried to readjust ourselves to the new ways. They asked embarrassing questions of those who denied Christ in industry; they sent out prophets against the lovers of profit; they aligned the brotherhood of Christ against the new racial hatreds and distinctions, they preached the leveling spirit against the formation of social clans and cliques. They matched Christ against the world.

The preaching of peace, however, was their prime concern, as it had always been. The Peace Association put lecturers into the field and poured out a stream of literature against war; there was a monthly magazine, *The Messenger of Peace,* and up at Lake Mohonk there was a yearly gathering of jurists, statesmen and lay friends of peace from all over the world. They talked of peace at Mohonk, of how to forestall Mars should he appear again. They were the chief agency engaged in spreading the gospel of international arbitration as a substitute for war; they were the leaders in the peace movement when the peace movement was at its best. They protested against the Spanish-American War; they condemned the war in the Philippines which followed it; they spoke out sharply against the fighting of British and Boer in South Africa. The fighting went on, in spite of them, as fighting always has. But they had done as George Fox ordered, as Christ had commanded. They could have done no more.

Came the revolver shot at Sarejevo in 1914, and their protesting was done for a while as the whole world went to war. Some of the Quakers went this time; some took arms, put on the uniform, went up on the firing step. Some others refused to go, went instead to Alcatraz, found themselves abused and humiliated according to the historic pattern. But not many, for the world was wiser in its treatment of the Quaker than it had ever been before. The warring nations, on the whole, were fairly easy on the Quaker objector. It had good reason to be. The Quaker was fighting for peace with better weapons than Mars', working hard to bring armistice while others were thinking only of gas for shells and petrol for bombers.

The Quaker was fighting for peace before America entered the fray. Five thousand dollars a month went overseas to British Quakers before we went in, to help along the work with war victims and refugees, with interned aliens and native conscientious objectors. When the President called for war and volunteers, the Friends were ready. They went to France, to Flanders, to Russia. They went without rifles or bayonets or hand grenades. They went with hoes, rakes, shovels, tractors, ambulances, as doctors, nurses, kindergarten teachers, carpenters, plumbers, farmers. They moved into ruined, ravaged towns after the armies had gone on, rebuilding houses, serving soup, nursing shell-shocked civilians, caring for the aged, nursing newborn babies with the rumble of cannon for lullaby. While tanks were cruising in no man's land with skull and crossbones painted on their sides, tractors were plowing the fields of bewildered peasants with the name *"Les Amis"* stenciled above the treads. *Les Amis!* The Friend of the friendless, of the French peasant and the German prisoner, while this tide of blood rose higher. In the Valley of the Marne, a Quaker boy and a German prisoner and a French poilu on leave reaped a harvest and stored it in a peasant's barn. *Les Amis!* There were dentists, surgeons, printers, opticians, farmers who pushed their plows so close to the heels of retreating or advancing armies that they ran on shells buried in the ground and left behind! They stocked farms with rabbits, chickens, sheep. They were busy rebuilding the world before the world had stopped falling.

They did not fight. They loved. They administered a fund of thirty million dollars in Germany alone from 1916 to 1919; they spent this fortune feeding the children of "the enemy"; they put free Christian bread in the mouths of every one of a dozen boys who some years later were to take their places in the cabinet of dictator Hitler as enemies of the Christian Church! They took coal and milk to Vienna when coal and milk had become prewar myths. There were feeding stations and first-aid stations in Russia before and after the Revolution, before Lenin got his grip, before the Soviet turned on the Church.

And when the need for feeding stations was gone, they worked on. In the same war areas they stayed on, preaching peace, good will, brotherhood. They maintained "peace embassies," good-will centers, at Paris, Vienna, Moscow, Berlin. They settled down again to the job of educating for peace. They're still at it.

They put us to shame. We have not yet appreciated them. They have been the salt of the earth. They were the logical result of the Protestant Reformation, the rebirth of New Testament Christianity. We have sold God cheaply, time and again, on the auction blocks of Mammon; they have sacrificed the spoils of Mammon and kept the Voice. We have denied the Prince of Peace continuously in a never-ending theatrical of war; they have been trying, almost alone, to drive war from off the earth. We are pacifists now; they have always been pacifists. We pass solemn resolutions now against Mars and all his works and think we are brave; the Quaker has been doing that for two hundred and fifty years. What is more, he has had the Christian courage to stand by his solemn resolutions, when war broke over his head.

Before the rest of us knew anything was wrong, the Quaker was pioneering in charity, in social justice and reform. He pleaded for the insane when we bound them in miles of chain; he begged for better prisons when not one in ten thousand of the rest of us knew what the inside of a prison looked like, or cared. He championed the slave when the world thrived on slave labor. He befriended the Indian when others called him heathen, savage, brute and beast. He was tolerant when we thought tolerance was sin. He has been gracious, gentle, Christian. He might have made the world a brotherhood, had we given him half a chance.

And how was he able to do all this? Not by way of politics nor with the aid of politicians; he early deserted the political arena and he has had few friends at court. Not by dint of numbers, for he has only one hundred thousand members in America. The secret of his power lies elsewhere. In his calm soul. In his deep, meditating heart. In his Inner Light. What wonders hath God wrought with that Light! It has cleansed, purified, illuminated us. Out of that limitless individual Quaker devotion to the Light and the Voice within has come the most amazing and far-reaching social advance that the world has known. They have been true and it has followed as the night the day . . .

The world cries for lost peace; the Quaker has it. The world is turning back to study the way of Jesus as a way out; the Quaker has long walked in that way. The world bemoans its modern, endless crucifying of the Nazarene; but since the man in leather breeches came crying "Woe!" to Lichfield, the Quakers have been reaching up to draw the nails from the torn and bleeding hands and feet.   And with the Victim of the world's madness on His cross, they have overcome the world.

THE METHODISTS

CHAPTER X

THE METHODISTS

(I)

YOUNG Reverend John Wesley knew he was a failure
in 1729, a failure at twenty-six. He'd made a mess of
things at Wroote, where he had been pastoral assistant
to his father, Samuel Wesley, Rector of Epworth. He
hadn't been of much assistance; his sermons fell flat and
his flock didn't seem to understand him. Maybe he was
too young; maybe they thought of him as a downy-
cheeked youngster trying to advise his elders. Too bad!
His friends had thought John Wesley would do something
in the Church; he'd had a brilliant record at Oxford,
where he had been elected a Fellow of Lincoln, no mean
honor. But as a pastor, no. He just didn't fit. So, come
November of '29, he packed his bags and slammed the
door of the rectory and went back up to Oxford. At
least he was a Fellow there, with a job he liked and a
little prestige.

He unpacked his bags and set up his books and joined
a new club. A foolish little club it was, with half a dozen
members; his brother Charles Wesley was one of them

and there was a big strapping fellow, the son of an innkeeper of Gloucester, who went by the name of George
Whitefield and who was working his way through college waiting tables. They were, said the campus, a fra-
ternity of fools. They met to talk about religion! They
mooned around about reaping the harvest of the Lord
while the regular fellows were sowing their wild oats;
they drank in "the Word" while the red-blooded regu-
lars were drinking porter and ale. They drew up a set
of rules for living, a set of rules and regulations which
covered everything and disciplined every waking hour.
They slept, rose, bathed, prayed, breakfasted, studied,
meditated, by the clock, according to schedule; they
gave most of their money (above bare living expenses)
to the needy and they visited the sick and the prisoners
and they taught the children of the poor to figure and
spell and read the Good Book; they kept all the commandments of the Word and the rubrics of the Church
as faithfully as monks in a monastery. Fools. Crack-
pots, with religion on the brain. Reforming Club.
Enthusiasts. Bible Moths. That's what the campus
called them. One undergraduate described them thus:

> "By rule they eat, by rule they drink,
> Do all things else by rule, but think—
> Accuse their priests of loose behaviour,
> To get more in the laymen's favor;
> Method alone must guide them all,
> Whence Methodists themselves they call."

Methodists! That was a nickname, an epithet, but John Wesley liked it. Naturally, for John Wesley was the incarnation of method, the soul of system and schedule in living. He always had to have a rule and a reason for everything. Long ago, he had read Jeremy Taylor's *Holy Living and Dying* and had forced himself to live according to Jeremy's holy rules. He was *born* a Methodist; he belonged to this crowd, by nature. Birds of a feather ...

The club (they called themselves the Holy Club) was six years old when Wesley's father died; in that year young John met a General. He met General Oglethorpe, who was sending colonists to Georgia. The General sent the student to Georgia, to preach to the settlers and convert the noble Indian, to try out his Holy-Club ideas in the wilderness. With him sailed Brother Charles and Benjamin Ingham. On the ship he met a company of Moravians, whose piety and courage he first admired, then imitated.

Georgia didn't like him. He was too strict, too churchy, too much of a sacramentarian, too severe in a land where life was loose and cheap and easy. He could do nothing with the "noble" Indian, whom he soon came to despise. He lost ground with Oglethorpe when he preached against slavery; he called slavery "the sum of all villainies" and the General disagreed; Oglethorpe considered any criticism of slavery as "an interference with property rights." Wesley lost his last shred of authority over the colonists when he bungled a love affair with Miss Sophia Hopkey and refused to serve her at communion after she had married another. (Unlucky at love was John Wesley; when he finally married, he found himself wed to a vixen, a terror, a shrew that would have made the heart of a Shakespeare leap and glow.) It was a comedy of errors; it was the end of Wesley in Georgia. His Methodism was a failure. Disgusted, he sailed for home in 1738.

Can you see him walking the streets of London, head down, hands behind him, wandering, disconsolate, ashamed? One failure at twenty-six, another at thirty-five. Why was he so futile? Why this constant defeat? He talked to Peter Böhler about it; Böhler was one of those Moravians and Böhler said to him, "My brother, your philosophy must be purged away. . . ." What Wesley needed was a little less method and a little more conviction; he was going in too much for the sacraments, too little for conversion and Christian experience; he needed a quiet Moravian conversion; how could he save the souls of others, unless he was sure of his own? Get right with God first, John Wesley! Böhler went on to America; John Wesley went to a prayer meeting and got right with God.

He went to a prayer meeting in Aldersgate Street, in London; it was the evening of May 24, 1738. He dropped in and sat there quietly; the leader was reading from Martin Luther's *Epistle to the Romans;* Wesley listened, moodily. All of a sudden, Wesley never knew how, the truth he had been searching for flashed upon him; heaven exploded into view before his eyes. "At about a quarter to nine," says John Wesley, "while he (the leader) was describing the change which God works in the heart through faith in Christ, I felt my heart strangely warmed. I felt I did trust in Christ, Christ alone for salvation; and an assurance was given me that he hath taken away my sins, even mine, and saved me from the law of sin and death." There you have it. That's Methodism, with the dross burned out. It comes down to this: Methodism is a heart-warming experience. Methodism is a tremendous institution built upon a tremendous proposition; the institution has nine million members; the proposition is that all men, *all* men, sin and need saving from the penalties, the death of sin, need to have their hearts warmed by the blazing presence of Christ, need to be fortified with the assurance that "he hath taken away my sins, even mine. . . ." The theme song of two hundred years of Methodism has been *"Blessed Assurance, Jesus Is Mine"*; or has it been *"Saved, Saved, Saved to the Uttermost"*? Methodism may have had its start in Oxford's Holy Club, but it rests its case at last on a prayer meeting in Aldersgate Street and on the frail shoulders of a tubercular Oxford graduate who had failed twice by thirty-five but who after Aldersgate knew what was the matter with him and with England and with Georgia and with the world.

He couldn't keep it to himself; no man with an experience like that has ever been able to keep it to himself. He had to tell others, to help other hearts get warm. He ran to Brother Charles with the good news and they wept together; Charles had already been warmed. He ran to Peter Böhler and Peter rejoiced with him and advised him to organize a society to guard it and spread it; not another Church, but just a society within the Church of England. He ran back from Peter to London, to Fetter Lane, where he gathered together seven of the old Oxford Methodists and three score new laymen for a "love feast" on New Year's Day of 1739. They prayed till three in the morning. He ran back to the Church of England, where he was still an ordained priest, to tell them about it. The Church of England slammed its doors in his face.

That was hard, for Wesley loved that Church. He had not the least intention of breaking away from it. Indeed, he never did break with it, nor take anyone from it; those who followed him, for the most part, were never *in* the Anglican Church. All he wanted to do was what all great church reformers have always wanted to do: to purify, enliven the Church from within. Right here, he met trouble. There were many in the high places of the Church who saw no need for purification or new life;

they were satisfied. Why upset things? Let well enough alone. But Wesley couldn't. He was an "enthusiast" for Christ now and he could not be still, and an enthusiast was about as popular in that Church as a bomb-throwing anarchist is in the White House. Opposition challenged, sharpened him; he went on until, one after another, he found all London's pulpits closed against him. He shook the dust of that city from his feet and went down to Bristol, where George Whitefield, after the old Holy Club manner, had been holding open-air revivals. He found closed pulpits in Bristol, too. So, at Whitefield's urging, he went out to a high mound near Kingswood and preached a sermon to anyone who would come. His text was, "The Spirit of the Lord is upon me, because he hath appointed me to preach the gospel to the poor . . . to heal the broken hearted . . . to set at liberty them that are bruised. . . ." It was the text of Jesus' sermon to the poor of Nazareth and it was Methodism's Declaration of Independence.

The poor! Three-quarters of England wallowed in poverty, lived in hovels and fought over crusts, worked unbelievably cruel hours in mill, factory and shop and went maudlin drunk at night, on gin, trying to forget; the other one-quarter was the rich, despotic, godless, heartless moneyed class that swung the whip. The bruised! Women and children worked the mines, crawling in the dark on bleeding knees, torn, cut, bruised, dead and dying. To set at liberty! Boys were being hung for stealing shoes, widows for stealing bread, the jails were jammed and crime was increasing and Dick Turpin was riding on the London road. The broken-hearted? It was England's heart that was broken, England's humanity and morale. It was the darkest hour of her darkest night; morality was dying, religion had taken wings and flown away, no one seemed to know where God was, the submerged three-quarters were locked in the dungeons of the Giant Despair and their masters, the money barons, were asking brazenly, "What are you going to do about it?"

And here comes John Wesley, ready to do something. He's five feet six inches tall and he weighs one hundred and twenty pounds; he's tubercular and he's been a failure twice and he's been frozen out of the church of his fathers. The parsons hate him, for he is an enthusiast; the rich laymen hate him, for he is stirring up the people. But the submerged three-quarters hear him gladly; they stand by hundreds, thousands, tens of thousands; they are the hosts of those who have turned away from the smug parsons who "said their prayers with the aid of a T-square," who preached on Sabbath morning from the text, "Be not righteous overmuch" and who were dead drunk by three on Sabbath afternoon. He preaches standing on his father's tombstone; he preaches in taverns, horsefairs, jails, mining pits, on street corners.

He talks their language; he never preaches over their heads; he paints the picture of their sinning and he offers them release; he tells them Christ wants them to come back. Men just out of the mine pits fall to weeping and the tears make wide white tracks down their grimy cheeks; slatternly women grip their children and stare hard. Repent, and come Home! Leave off the sin that has made you what you are. Let Christ warm your cold aching hearts. Hand over your burdens to the Burden-bearer and stand forth free and proud and strong. Behold the Lamb of God! Once he was asked to preach to a "fashionable" congregation in a "fashionable" church; he preached to them from the text, "Ye serpents, ye generation of vipers, how can *ye* *e*scape the damnation of hell?" He humbled the proud and he lifted the meek and he made each love the other. It was a reformation, a revival; it was England's second birth.

He did it not alone; he had help. George Whitefield helped; it was George Whitefield, the innkeeper's son, who led the way out into the open fields, who urged the employment of laymen as preachers; he was a pathfinder. He was often at odds with John Wesley, for theirs were conflicting skills and temperaments. Whitefield was the flaming orator, the foot-loose and restless agitator; Wesley was the quiet thinker, the organizer who nailed things down and pinned up the loose ends that Whitefield left flying. And brother Charles helped, too; he was the

singer, the Sankey of this British Awakening; he gave
it wings.   He wrote *Jesus, Lover of My Soul!*   Brother
John didn't care much for that hymn, but there must
have been a deal of comfort in it for the hosts of the submerged when they sang,

> "Other refuge have I none;
> Hangs my helpless soul on thee!"

He wrote "Oh, for a thousand tongues to sing!"   And
he wrote

> "My God is reconciled,
> His pardoning voice I hear . . ."

There were other hymns from the songbird, but these
have outlived the years; there were other preachers and
singers, in this Reformation, but these three were the
leaders: Whitefield gave it thunder, John Wesley gave
it sense, Charles gave it melody.

John Wesley bought a horse and he rode, rode from
Land's End to John o' Groat's, from Cork to London-
derry.   He faced sleet and rain and mud and mobs and
bitterness; he was mobbed in Wednesbury, but he got
two recruits for Methodism before he left, a young man
named Francis Asbury and another named Richard
Whatcoat.   Mobs and parsons soon gave it up; Wesley's
march through the towns of England became one long

march of triumph. He rode five thousand miles a year, preached forty-two thousand sermons in fifty years; he was a traveling preacher, a circuit-rider, an itinerant. He left behind him a string of schools and orphanages and widows' homes and medical dispensaries and Strangers' Societies; a most versatile and wide-horizoned man was this John Wesley. He gave a spiritual drive to the fight on slavery and alcohol, both of which he hated as he hated Satan; he fought the fight of the laboring man against the capitalist; he preached a social gospel as well as individual conversion. He did on a larger scale what George Fox had done: he preached an inner, personal salvation, knowing that social salvation would come out of that. If he could save men, he could save society. It worked, as it has always, must always, work. He gave England the most widespread social and economic and political revolution in all her history. He warmed England's heart and the rest followed as a matter of course.

In 1767 there were 22,410 Methodists in England, 2,801 in Ireland, 800 in Scotland and Wales. They were not a church; they were organized into "societies," and then into smaller "classes." They held "class meetings" under the guidance of "class leaders," in which they confessed their sins and tried to lift one another toward the cross. There were *lay* preachers, unordained but inspired and able to lead. There were preachers traveling from one society to another, itinerants, circuit-riders.

They gathered for a conference in 1744, at the Foundery (it was an old ruined iron foundry and cannon factory, in London); in that old cannon shop was born the *institutional* Methodism of today.   By then, all the organizational furniture of Methodism had been moved in; there were classes and class meetings and class leaders, itinerants, circuit-riders, lay preachers and the Methodist Conference.

There was a Conference in Leeds in 1769, with John Wesley in the chair.   He put a startling question to his preachers: "We have a pressing call from our brethren in New York (who have built a meetinghouse) to come over and help them.   Who is willing to go?"   Joseph Pilmoor and Richard Boardman were willing to go; two months later Pilmoor stood on the steps of the Old State House in Philadelphia (we call it Independence Hall) and delivered a Methodist sermon.   A Methodist sermon, not the first.

Whitefield had already been preaching here; the booming George had followed Wesley into Georgia, and gone free-lancing for the Lord all up and down the coast, attracting thousands and leaving behind him an awareness of God and a statue of himself on the campus of the University of Pennsylvania.   Whitefield bridged the gap between Wesley's failure in Georgia and the coming of Pilmoor; no finer preacher than he has ever been heard on this side of the world.   But after all, he preached and

went away; the first Methodists to come and stay were
not from Whitefield's England, but from Ireland. They
were here by 1760; they were in New York and Maryland. Robert Strawbridge, fiery Celt, generous, two-
fisted and hard to get along with, built himself a log
cabin on Sam's Creek, in Frederick County, Maryland,
and invited his log-cabin neighbors in to a prayer meeting; he journeyed over eastern Maryland, Delaware,
Pennsylvania and Virginia, organizing "classes" and re-
cruiting ministers to spread his Methodist gospel; he got
hold of the first native Methodist preachers in America.
He did a lot of good and he got himself into a lot of
trouble. When he died, his bishop remarked that the Lord
had been kind in taking him away from Maryland! That
may be true; it is also true that fiery Irish Strawbridge
gave Methodism its first firm foothold in the South,
where it is still strong.

Up in New York, a band of Methodists had landed;
they had sailed from County Limerick. More Irish!
Among them was a young carpenter, a Methodist ex-
horter named Philip Embury, and his cousin, one Mrs.
Barbara Heck. They were a team built to play a great
game. Embury was sincere and slow, timorous and given
to blushing; Barbara Heck was a walking cyclone, quick,
determined, aggressive; wherever she went, something
happened. One day she walked into a group of men
gambling over a game of cards; she scattered them to the

four winds, hurled the cards into the open fireplace and rushed off to the home of Cousin Philip Embury with the words, "Brother Embury, you must preach to us, or we shall all go to hell." Embury stammered, fidgeted and preached; preached in his own house; preached later, as his congregation grew, in an old storeroom down back of the barracks of the British troops. He had no pews, no rose windows, no millionaires nor city fathers in his congregation; these were congregations like those Wesley had; they were the poor and brokenhearted, the sick who really needed a physician. Embury preached at the city almshouse and made good Methodists out of several of the inmates. Carpenters, paupers, hoi polloi meeting in an old storeroom. American Methodism!

One morning, as Embury was preaching, a captain from the barracks stalked down the aisle and took a seat. He was Captain Webb, on his Majesty's service; he had a scarlet coat, a green patch over one eye and a good army record. Webb had been at Braddock's defeat; he had been wounded in the arm and he had lost an eye at Louisburg and he had watched Wolfe die on the Plains of Abraham. And he had heard John Wesley preach. Wesley's words went deeper than the bullets; the captain began to preach wherever anyone would listen. Within a week he was preaching in New York, in green patch and coat of scarlet and with his old sword across the pulpit, preaching salvation from sin, calling in New York's sinners with the powerful bass that had sent men forth to die on the battlefield. Soon the storeroom was too small, and they moved down to a rigging loft in William Street. A rigging loft, where sails were cut and stitched, where the smell of tar and rope was in the air. What text did you preach from, one-eyed Webb? From Psalm 107, 23: "They that go down to the sea in ships, that do business in great waters . . ."?

So when Pilmoor stood forth on the steps of the Old State House, he already had an American Methodist background; the day he stepped ashore Captain Webb handed him a chart, or diagram, of the "American Circuit." What a circuit! There was hardly one good church building on it; there was no trained or ordained ministry, no money, no organization, no influence. There was only a string of Methodist prayer meetings from New York to Maryland, led by a carpenter, a one-eyed captain, a woman who hated cards and a fiery Irishman who kept breaking out of line. They were trying to establish themselves, to wedge themselves in between the stronger, well-established Anglicans, Baptists, Presbyterians, Lutherans, Dutch Reformed. Wedge; that's the word for it. The Methodists were a wedge. On the one hand was the Church of England, preaching salvation by sacrament and rubric; on the other hand were the Calvinistic churches, preaching salvation by election, gained effortlessly by the few and agonizingly out of reach for the many; in between them drifted the Methodist, preaching that anyone, everyone, might be saved by simple confession of faith in Christ, preaching to the outsiders, the unchurched. Methodism got the people who were dissatisfied with the extremes of Calvinists and Anglicans. It was slow work.

It was Barbara Heck who pushed through the first building project in New York and who gave American Methodism its first shrine; she prayed and raised the cash to build a chapel in John Street. Old John Street! There's a Methodist Church there now; it is a Methodist Mecca for those Americans who know their Church and love it. Embury supervised the building of that first chapel; he put in a fireplace and a chimney, to get around those Church of Englanders who forbade dissenters to build "regular" church buildings; then he built the pulpit with his own hands and preached from it the sermon of dedication. Cousin Barbara sat in the congregation; she put in an "Amen, brother!" now and then.

That was in 1768; already, the march south had begun. Webb and a Methodist "class" in Philadelphia bought a half-finished building from a group of discouraged German Reformers; Robert Williams came over from England, from Wesley, passed through Philadelphia on his way to Maryland, to help Strawbridge, to dip deeper into the South and to establish Methodism in Virginia and the Old Dominion. John King arrived in 1769 and introduced Methodism in Baltimore; he preached his first sermon in a blacksmith's shop, another from a tavern table. He faced a mob at the tavern; he shouted them down. John King was given to shouting; he may have been the first "shouting Methodist" in America. Once John Wesley wrote to him: "Scream no more, at the peril of your soul." Wesley hated shouting; he had no use for loud crying and emotion and hysteria in religion.

The American societies multiplied and Webb begged Wesley to send more preachers. Two more came out, at his call and bidding, in 1771. One was a failure, named Richard Wright; the other was the greatest Methodist ever to tread American soil. He was that convert gained by Wesley in the riot at Wednesbury; he was Francis Asbury, the Prophet of the Long Road, the pioneer circuit-rider, the unifier, the apostle who turned defeat into victory at the zero hour and built a church on catastrophe.

Asbury established headquarters in Philadelphia; Wright went to New York; Pilmoor turned southward and Boardman headed for New England. Thomas Rankin and George Shadford joined them, sent by Wesley. (Wesley wrote to Shadford, "I let you loose, George, on the great continent of America. Publish your message in the face of the open sun. . . .") Rankin was appointed superintendent of the work in America, over

Asbury; Asbury was hurt, but went on publishing. In 1773 they held the first American Methodist Conference in Philadelphia; there were ten of them, all told. Ten, to hold a territory stretching from Norfolk on the south to Boston on the north. But the true center of Methodism, right then, lay in the South. In 1735, there were 3,148 Methodists in the Colonies; 2,384 of them lived south of Mason and Dixon's Line. And south of that Line was the first progress made. A revival broke out in Virginia; Methodist preaching produced a "great shaking among the dry bones" and the whole south of Mason and Dixon's Line. And south of that Line was the first progress made. A revival broke been that these revivalistic cavalrymen were riding hardest just as Paul Revere was riding hard against the dawn in Massachusetts. The American Revolution broke up the Methodist revival. And it broke up the Methodists.

In the year that Lexington was fought, every English Methodist preacher save Francis Asbury left the country and Asbury went into retirement. Pilmoor, Boardman, Shadford, all of them sailed for England; only the untrained, native local preachers were left. Why? Well, Wesley had a lot to do with it. Wesley opposed the Revolution and condemned the rebels in the Colonies; John Wesley was an outspoken Tory and he didn't care who knew it. He wrote a "Calm Address to our American Colonies" that was anything but calm, which did much to influence the British public mind against the Americans and to turn the Americans against the Methodists. And when the Wesleyan preachers in America fell to preaching political sermons and distributing the "Calm Address" they scuttled their own ship; every Methodist became a suspected Loyalist, a potential Tory until he proved himself a good rebel. The Methodists, as such, nearly disappeared. Some of them, providentially, left the war area of the eastern coast and fell back into the western wilderness, where they waited, like runners on their mark, for the push west after Yorktown.

There they were when the peace was signed in 1783, disorganized, leaderless, smashed. There was Asbury, just out of hiding and with a handful of local preachers. What could they do now? Better quit and forget it, Methodists; quit it and go back to the Established Church, where you belong. It was hopeless. The father of the movement was a Tory in England and he'd better stay there and keep his Tory preachers there with him. America wanted none of them. Asbury had no right to ordain a fresh crop of Methodist preachers. It was a Gordian knot. Wesley cut it.

John Wesley, God bless him, saw the handwriting on the wall. He saw that either American Methodism must have a body of regular, recognized clergymen, or American Methodism would die in its cradle. So he called in a Dr. Thomas Coke to his study, explained to him that the Americans needed a whole new church government, an *episcopal* form of government, and that he proposed, immediately, to ordain Doctor Coke himself to be the first American bishop. Coke hesitated; he was a good Anglican and there was no precedent for this. No, agreed Wesley, but there was a need, a crisis. It ended by Wesley laying his hands on Coke's head. The same day, he ordained Richard Whatcoat (he of Wednesbury!) and Thomas Vasey as ministers to help the rather bewildered "bishop." Two months later the three walked down the gangplank in New York.

Across the Colonies, like wildfire, went the news of their coming. Coke rode a thousand-mile circuit to meet his preachers; Freeborn Garretson leaped into the saddle and "went like an arrow over North and South," calling them in to a Conference. The Conference, said the flying Freeborn, would be held in Baltimore; it would open the day before Christmas. It was 1784.

They met in Lovely Lane ("lane," you know, is a polite name for an alley) on the water front. Preacher John Dickens made a motion; he moved that they in Conference assembled form here and now a Methodist Episcopal Church. Why not? Coke had been made a bishop in anticipation of just that. It was moved, seconded and carried. The Methodist Episcopal Church!

Remember, there was no such church in England, or anywhere else; there were only Methodist "societies" within another church. It was the height of Christian audacity for them to do that; it took the courage of the impossible, or the courage of the fool. Or both.

By acclamation, they elected Francis Asbury a bishop, to work with Coke. Up until then, Asbury had been only an itinerant preacher. On Christmas Day, on Christ's birthday, Coke called him up to the altar rail and made him a deacon; the next day he called him forward again and made him an elder; the next, he laid his hands upon his head and called him bishop. Fast work; faster than it has ever been done, before or since. But what of that? Back of the fast three days lay years of slow, grueling labor in the wilderness. Asbury had earned it!

Look at them. Sixty preachers singing in a Baltimore alley! Ecclesiastically speaking, they were interlopers, pretenders; to the strict churchman they had no rights, as preachers, whatsoever; they were a pack of arrogant rebels who had dared ordain themselves to the holy work of God, who went so far as to set up their own bishops without benefit of precedent. They called themselves a church; they had mighty few steeples, fewer pews and nary a hymn book to a thousand of them; their total membership was two thousand and seventy-six, and half of them were in one state, Maryland. Sixty preachers, trying to do something with that! Sixty preachers who were poor. And uneducated. And young.

They sang one last hymn, prayed one last prayer together, shook hands like brave men shaking hands as the bugle sounds an impossible "Charge," turned their backs on Lovely Lane and melted into the black Baltimore night. In the morning, Baltimore did not even know that they had gone.

CHAPTER XI

THE METHODISTS

(II)

ENERGETIC Bishop Coke made a bad mistake in the General Conference of 1796; with his episcopal authority as a lever, he tried to push through a resolution the preacher-delegates didn't like. When one objected, Coke flared, "Do you think yourself equal to me?" To which another slightly brazen preacher-rebel replied: "We do think ourselves equal to him, notwithstanding that he was educated at Oxford . . . and more than that, we think ourselves equal to Doctor Coke's king." The Bishop withdrew his resolution.

That episode is a window through which we may catch a revealing glimpse of early American Methodism. It tells something of the dictatorial temper of the first bishops and it explains why the Methodist Episcopal Church managed to stay alive through the crucial days after Lovely Lane. Men with nerve enough to talk back to a bishop in that day would have nerve enough to attempt most anything; which they had and which they did. They rode circuits fifty miles square, sixty, seventy, eighty. They preached from stumps in the woods when they lacked polished pulpits; they had an abundance of zeal to balance their lack of learning. They had no help, no money or men, from England, when they needed it most; but they had a few young Americans, free, stalwart, fearless, with a great future somewhere down the road. And they had Francis Asbury.

He was their leader; they felt his power and they followed him as the Old Guard followed Napoleon. Down the Road he led them, on forced marches toward the future they never doubted; out ahead of them he rode, scouting, picking sites for church-fortresses, establishing garrisons, saying, "You preach here," or "You go there." He rode and rode and rode, rode through fifteen states from Georgia to Maine and back again and back and back. He crossed the Ohio, waded the Watauga, mounted the highlands of the Hudson. Rode, rode, rode, rode farther than Wesley; he could do four hundred miles in twenty days, he did two hundred and seventy-five thousand miles before death cornered him. He was Methodism's man in the saddle, the tireless itinerant, the Prophet of the Long Road, forging out a church that should forever love and follow the Road. Swamps, rivers, mountains, sleet and wilderness. His horse fell on him, he was lost in a swamp and caught in a whirlpool and a bandit creased his cheek with a bullet. Rode, rode, rode. He slept on log-cabin floors, he slept in the mud, he fell asleep in the saddle; he made one hundred miles in two days in Kentucky and did not sleep at all. He preached sin and salvation and getting saved and taking Christ; he prayed. How he prayed! He advised, inspired, dictated, blessed, wept often and smiled almost never and burned himself out on the Road. He preached his last sermon propped up in a chair in 1816. The day of his funeral there were seven hundred ordained Methodist preachers in the fifteen states he had covered and two hundred thousand members in a Methodist Episcopal Church who knew at last how strong they were and what they had to do. Dead? Asbury never died. Methodists still follow the footprints of his horse, there in the Road.

Asbury followed the shifting frontier as the road wound over the Alleghenies; he followed the wagons into the woods. In the woods he found "poor preachers indifferently clad, with emaciated bodies." Some of them were riding circuits four hundred miles long, and liking it; they got eighty dollars per year and "traveling expenses" (oats for the horse); being graduates of nothing better than Hardscrabble University and Brush College, they said "ain't" occasionally. They preached often at camp meeting. Draw a red circle here: the camp meeting was an all-important factor in the molding of the nation. It was not strictly a Methodist institution, but Methodists loved it; it was their method of following

the trek across the mountains and of evangelizing the
frontier. Camp meetings, usually, were held in the
woods; a great clearing was hacked out, tents pitched
in a circle around it, platforms thrown up for the
preachers and planks laid across the stumps for the worshipers. Sermons lasted for hours; often six or seven
sermons were going at once. The exhorters whipped
up their hearers into a frenzy, into yelps of fear as they
excoriated the gambling, drinking, gun fighting, God-
forsaking sin of their frontier that was dragging them
straight to the brink of hell. Men sobbed, women
fainted, children writhed and jerked in white-faced fear;
sinners fell in rows, like cut wheat, before the preachers'
scythes; one witness claims he saw "at least five hundred
hurled down in a moment, as if a battery of a thousand
guns had opened upon them." They dropped on piles
of straw, placed for their falling. The congregation
encouraged them to come and fall with a lively tune:

"The troops of Hell are mustering round, Hallelujah!
But Zion still is gaining ground, O Glory, Hallelujah!"

And when they fell came the glad shouting chorus:

"Shout, shout, we're gaining ground, Hallelujah!
We'll shout old Satan's kingdom down, Hallelujah!"

Crude? Yes. Why not? What was not crude, then?
Asbury made one preaching tour protected by an armed

guard; bluff old Peter Cartwright, the great camp-meeting preacher who came later and who ran against Abraham Lincoln for Congress, had to be as quick with his fists as with his Scripture; it was a day of catch-as-catch-can wrestling with fierce border deviltry. Crude or no, the camp meeting saved the frontier from becoming a devil's happy hunting ground. It brought together the far-flung circuit-riders and made them see their job with one eye and one heart; it gathered in the scattered settlers, gave them release for long-pent emotions, a sense of individual mastery over their lonesome souls and a sense of their social sins. And it left the frontier dotted with churches.

By now, the Methodists were thoroughly organized. Coming so tardily and having so little to work with, they were the first church in America to work out an independent and strictly national organization. The system they built is still at work, with but little change. At the bottom are the *Quarterly* Conferences, in the local church, where the pastor reports to the district superintendent on his work, yearly; pastors of certain geographical areas are grouped into *Annual* Conferences, presided over by a bishop who assigns the pastors to their charges; at the top is the *General* Conference, which meets every four years, which makes the rules and elects the bishops. In 1808 General Conference made a bishop of William McKendree, known as "Major-General

McKendree" because he was virtually in command of the great region west of the Alleghenies, and as "the Lion of the West," for he was king of the preachers and strongest of them all. McKendree was the greatest administrator this Church ever produced; he was the man who gave the Methodists a constitution and a constitutional way of doing things and who thereby set them free from the old dictatorial Episcopacy of Asbury and Coke. He made Methodism democratic.

The Road was winding on, meanwhile, toward the Pacific; the Methodists followed it. In 1803 a lone circuit-rider turned up in Illinois; 1806, and a saddle-bags parson was riding Mad Anthony Wayne's old road across Indiana. Mississippi and Tennessee saw preachers trailing the wagon trains; they penetrated Ohio, Michigan, Alabama, Florida, down into the Louisiana country, southwest to Texas, northwest to Oregon, where Jason Lee preached to the Blackfeet and helped bring that state into the Union. The first prospector to sink a pick in Colorado found a Methodist itinerant at his elbow; those who washed gold in Sutter's Creek heard sermons on Sunday from the text, "Ye cannot serve God and mammon." That was as far west as he could go; the Pacific was too deep for his horse to swim and he sat disconsolately in the saddle, half resentful that there were no more worlds for him to conquer, staring across the briny barrier toward China and Japan.

But the germ of an idea boiled in his mind as he sat there, an idea called "missions," an idea implanted by a man named John Stewart. John Stewart was a Negro who had staggered, drunk, into a camp meeting and walked away sober and possessed of a dream. He thought God was calling him to preach to the Indians along the Road; he dipped into the forest and opened his Bible in the wigwams of the Wyandottes and the Delawares. McKendree backed him. A Negro, preaching to red-skins, supported by white gold. Perfect! That's the spirit of Methodist missions. It was not long before the first Methodist Missionary and Bible Society was formed to send more preachers with Bibles after John Stewart in the forest, to the Creeks and the Cherokees, the Choctaws, Onandagas, Mohawks. The first messenger of the Society went to the French in Louisiana; a host of them went to the Negro. That's perfect, too.

Now that word "missions" stuck in the mind of the Methodist as he sat there in his saddle at the western edge of the sea. Why not missions over there beyond the horizon? Why not leave the saddle for the clipper ship? As he pondered a voice came from the sea mists, and a finger beckoned; the voice and the finger of Thomas Coke, who had gone sailing to India to preach years before and who had died on the way and been buried at sea. Now Coke called. Come on, come on! There are more, more, more waiting to be saved, multitudes

in the East waiting in the valley of decision. In 1832
Melville Cox went to Liberia. Melville Cox had
tuberculosis and he went *there*. He signed his own
death warrant when he went; he was dead within four
months' time; he wrote home to the Society: "Let a
thousand fall before Africa be given up." Five stepped
into his place. Fifty years later, there were only twenty-
three hundred converts in Liberia. What of that? Men
went down to South America, saw their mission stations
rise and fall like rockets in the night, fought and died
against the most deadly opposition any cause has ever
known. What of that? The rockets kept going up,
however great the opposition or scant the fruits, and at
last the pagan world saw them and took heart. William
Taylor was the first great Methodist missionary success;
"California Taylor," they called him; he had preached
to the 'forty-niners on the San Francisco docks. He
also did some preaching to Kaffirs in the African bush,
established a string of self-supporting missions in India
and got himself elected Bishop of Africa. On his heels
came Thoburn, who also knew his lean years, but who
started at last a mass movement in India which swept in
thousands, whole villages and towns, for Christ. He
built a great church building, capacity sixteen hundred,
with twenty-one dollars donated by a widow as a start;
he filled it. He specialized in Eurasians (half-caste, half
European, half Indian). Then his sister, Isabella, came

out to help him; she specialized in another unwanted slice of Indian society: the women. Against a passive opposition that would have broken a Hercules and discouraged a Francis, she opened a school for women in Lucknow; today it is the Isabella Thoburn College. Today one Indian out of every eighty-six is a Christian. Think it over, all ye in the modern Church at home who are "discouraged" in these "hard times." There were no such words as these in the Thoburn dictionary.

Back home, there were some new Methodist colleges. Odd, that Methodists should be going in for colleges. Peter Cartwright once compared an educated preacher with "a gosling that has got the straddles from wading in the dew." One young fellow (later a bishop) was twice refused admission to a Conference because he wore good clothes and spoke good English! All that was changing now. The Methodists built Cokesbury College in 1787; that burned to the ground. They tried again with Asbury College, in Baltimore, which died speedily from "want of money and from a mongrel religion." Another, in Kentucky, lasted twenty-nine years and then it passed; they named it for ex-President Madison, but it died just the same. The first permanent schools were elementary schools, academies, seminaries; the first permanent college was Wesleyan, in Connecticut, the mother college of Methodism in the North, and Randolph-Macon, the mother of all southern. Then came Dickinson, Allegheny, McKendree, Indiana Asbury, Emory, Trinity (now Duke), Wofford and Central. All this in twenty years, from 1820 to 1840!

Missions and colleges: these were the bright spots of the era; there were black spots, for relief. There were creaks and rattles developing in the Methodist machine. James O'Kelley of Virginia threw a wrench into the gears when he attempted to check the power of the bishops; they had too much power in appointing preachers, said O'Kelley, and the preachers should have the right of appeal to the Conference and another appointment, if the Conference agreed. O'Kelley was voted down; he withdrew from the Church with a group (Freeborn Garretson and William McKendree were in sympathy with him) who set up the Republican Methodist Church. It didn't last very long; the O'Kelley rebellion was more of a warning than a storm. More serious was the deflection of the Reformers in 1821; the Reformers (good Methodists called them "radicals") withdrew in a fight over a proposition proposing the election of district superintendents and the admission of laymen to the Conferences. They formed the Methodist Protestant Church. That amounted to something. Today it has two hundred thousand members.

But the major catastrophe of American Methodism came in 1844; it was the split over slavery. The Methodists were not responsible for this division in their ranks; they were the "innocent drivers" in an accident thrust upon them by powerful forces of economic, political and social propaganda from without; the moral and religious aspects of that strife, whether we admit it or not, were deeply influenced by habits of life and economic situations on either side of Mason and Dixon's Line. Methodists in the agricultural South, born there, reared there, saw more good than harm in slavery; Methodists in the industrial North could see no good in it at all. For years, these opinions had been hardening, solidifying, enlarging. Veiled muttering at last broke within Methodism's house; the mutter became a roar in the General Conference of 1844, when the northerners challenged the right of Bishop Andrew of Georgia to remain a bishop. For Bishop Andrew, by marriage, had become a slaveholder. The northerners asked him to step aside; the southerners stood by him and went out en masse when the two forces came into a hopeless deadlock. They walked out, and formed the Methodist Episcopal Church, South. When Henry Clay heard of it, he cried, "My God. This means war!" It did. Twenty years later. Civil War.

The two Methodisms are with us yet, with separate equipments and organizations; in spite of repeated attempts to heal the old breach, it remains. Yet the picture is not a hopeless one. The two churches have a common hymnal, catechism and form of worship. The old causes of separation are long since dead and buried and the newer ones which the years have brought are losing ground every day. There is concrete evidence of this in the statement of Bishop John W. Moore, of the Church, South, before the Sesquicentennial Celebration of the Methodists in Baltimore, in 1934. Said the Bishop: "This is a very late day for denominational quibbling, a very late day for sectional differences, a very late day for sectional sufficiencies." Reading that, the reunion of Methodism seems just ahead.

Both Churches threw themselves into the Civil War. The Church South sent two hundred chaplains and lost two hundred and fifty thousand members out of a total of seven hundred thousand. The Church North, according to President Lincoln, sent "more soldiers to the field, more nurses to the hospitals, more prayers to heaven than any other (church)." It sent, to be exact, one hundred thousand soldiers, five hundred chaplains, four hundred and eighty-eight ministers to serve in the Christian Commission on the field. Naturally, the Church North recovered faster, when the fighting was over.

It recovered with a rush, thanks to that old Methodist habit of rising smiling out of ruin. In a burst of getting and spending, it staged a Centenary Celebration (commemorating the founding of American Methodism in

1766), raised nine million dollars and spent it on missions, new churches and new schools. They built two churches a day for a while, till the money ran out, and they built yet more great colleges: Syracuse, Boston, Southern California, Hamline, Vanderbilt, Denver, Goucher. In a fresh burst of republicanism, they admitted laymen to General Conference (in 1872) and even started an agitation to admit women! It took another thirty years for the ladies to get in, for the idea that "woman's place is in the home" was so strong that even gallant Frances Willard was denied a seat in General Conference!

They sent more teachers southward now, to the four million liberated Negroes, to rescue them from the wiles of the despicable carpetbagger; the Freedman's Aid Society was at work in 1866, teaching black men, women and children to read and spell and write and count. One-quarter of a million Negroes have since passed through the schools of higher learning which evolved from those first Freedman's Aid elementary schools. Today there are four flourishing colored Methodist churches, with their own preachers, bishops and organizations.

These same years saw John H. Vincent and the Epworth League. The League was formed in Cleveland, in 1889; it is the young people's department of the Methodist Episcopal Church and a vital part of its work. John H. Vincent worked with young people too; with people younger than Leaguers, with Sunday-School pupils. He revolutionized the Sunday School, in more denominations than the Methodist, by popularizing Bible study with the Uniform Lessons, by leading the way in teacher-training institutes and assemblies. Out on the shores of lovely Lake Chautauqua (originally a Methodist camp-meeting ground), he started a teacher's assembly which with the years grew up into a great American institution: *the* Chautauqua.

Thus far, the Methodists had run well and fought a good fight. They had rescued beleaguered souls from Satan with their camp meeting; reclaimed the Negro from the bondage of King Cotton; snatched captives from King Dunce with their schools and colleges. What now? Who next? Where would the Road lead them now, and to what? It led to fresh adventure and romance in quarters unsuspected; it led them up to the saloon, the factory and the sweatshop, to the battlefields where men in arms went out needlessly to die and to the fighting ground where races clashed. It was a sharp turn in the Road, in the Methodist temper. For years they had been most intent upon conversion, upon the life eternal, upon a future heaven and a hell to come. Now they discovered afresh that heaven and hell were all about them, here and now; now they saw clearly that this life is a part of eternity. Heaven? That was a condition, not a place; men need not wait for death to usher them in to Christ in his Kingdom of Heaven; men who loved Christ and did His commandments were living in heaven on this earth! Hell? There was plenty of it, along the Road; men were living and dying in a hellish sort of helplessness, hopelessness; legions of the lost were wallowing in the swamps of despair, denied a chance to walk or even see the Christ. That was hell. The Methodists decided to wipe it off the earth. Not that they planned to turn from their old conversion emphasis, nor to forget God in Heaven; they still put their trust in Him, in that, and laid their course for His courts of Glory. But they put a sharper eye on the terribly earthy earth their feet must tread to get there; they would, they said, rear up Heaven right on the Road. They would drive from it those things and tendencies and anti-Christian errors which made men take their minds off God; they would help men to get converted and to stay converted by Christianizing the environment in which men had to live. It was a new militant Methodism still holding fast to the tenet that men needed to be saved, about to start building a saved society.

They struck first at the most violent enemy of the Christian way of life that they could find: they struck at alcohol. From Wesley down to their own day, they had discovered alcohol to be a Circe's wand changing potential saints to pitiful sots; they would be rid of that, they vowed. They started preaching temperance; they circulated total abstinence pledges; their women prayed in the streets outside the saloon and (which was more effective) they jotted down the names of those who passed in through the swinging doors! They added insult to injury, the strength of organization to theory, by forming the W. C. T. U., with Frances Willard (our candidate for American Saint Number One), at its head and by supporting an Anti-Saloon League. (That League was never one hundred per cent Methodist, as many believe; it was all "the churches in action.") Drip, drip, drip went the drops of water on the Gibraltar of the liquor traffic. The traffic laughed—and went down! The fight for temperance evolved into the fight for legal, national prohibition and in 1918 came the Eighteenth Amendment. Think what you will of that amendment and its fall, but remember this: the slow drip, drip, drip of the new militant Methodism was instrumental in influencing ninety per cent of the land of this country and seventy per cent of the population to *vote itself dry before 1918*. So that amendment was hardly "sneaked across by a handful of Methodists." Maybe it will come back, maybe not; either way, until alcohol destroys us or we destroy it, you will find a Methodist chasing John Barleycorn up and down the Road.

In 1908, at the height of the fracas with the liquor

traffic, the Methodists invited more trouble into their house, this time from the industrialists, the militarists, the advocates of racial superiority and the whole world-wide anti-Christian social and economic order in one lump. They sent out the invitation in the form of a Social Creed of the Methodist Episcopal Church, the most daring document in the history of the Christian Church. It called attention to the inexcusable poverty that thrived in our world of plenty; to the injustices being loaded upon the backs of labor; to the murder of little children and the exploitation of women in industry, to low wages and consequent low-living standards. It demanded the Christianization of the world's social and economic life. As Doctor Luccock of Yale aptly phrased it, later, at the Baltimore Sesquicentennial, "It is no use to talk of saving souls and have no concern for a world that damns souls. The major task of religion is to control the machinery of our day so that it will not be the master of men, as it is so largely now, but their servant." That's what the Methodists have been fighting for, since the Social Creed of 1908. Every General Conference since then has repeated its determination in stronger and stronger language. The world can take it or leave it; that's where they stand.

The World War interrupted their campaign; they went to the war, fought it through and then, their bitter, bloody lesson learned in the futility of the war's

aftermath, they turned on war!   In 1924, General Conference went on record with this:

> "War is not inevitable. It is the supreme enemy of
> mankind.   We are determined to outlaw the whole
> war system."

Which means that the Methodists will not rush to the
next war as they did to the last.   They mean it.   They
have more pacifists in their pulpits than will be found
in the pulpits of any other denomination.

The same Conference of 1924 lashed out at race
prejudice,   at   Nordic   superiority   and   Nordic
imperialism:

> "We repudiate the idea that certain races are born
> to inherent and fixed superiority and rulership
> while others are born to inherent and fixed in-
> feriority and subordination.   We stand for the life
> of open opportunity for all."

Working from that, they have practiced at home what
they have preached abroad; they are done with the
Kiplingesque fable of "the white man's burden" (which
more often is "the white man's thievery,") and they
are resolved that whatever keeps races apart and color
in conflict must go.

Race and color: the Methodists have defied them.
There is nothing racial nor national about the Methodist

Episcopal Church; it is a church of the Road, a church that has girdled the earth. Their preachers preach in nineteen countries, preach of brotherhood and love and the common Fatherhood; their teachers teach grammar, language, Bible, philosophy, dentistry, medicine, agriculture, music, art. The little school that Isabella Thoburn started in a small room in Lucknow, with six pupils at her first session, has grown to a system of twelve hundred schools and over fifty thousand pupils. Untouchables and rajahs, mandarins and coolies, watching that growth, have watched the barriers go down, caste go, old customs and ancient superstitions go as Methodist missions have multiplied; they know in their hearts that a new day has come, a day in which world-brotherhood is mounting a throne of world power. The Methodists have not done it alone, but they have had a leading part. They have embraced the world in one of the most intrepid missionary efforts that the world has ever known.

Abroad and at home, they have, at one time or another, been considered outlaws. Outlaws! That fits them. They have been that since they began, with outlaw John Wesley; their teachings were propagated, in their earliest days, by men who were regarded widely as so many British soldiers and tavernkeeper's sons, filled with social religious renegades, so many ecclesiastical rebels; their first pews were filled by the preaching of one-eyed outlaws, outcasts, lower-castes, untouchables, un-churched, untaught and undesirable.   Despised and rejected themselves, they turned to the despised and re-jected, turned from the noble halls of Oxford to ignoble hut and mining pit and cabin of logs where dwelled the humble folk who could not read or write but who could sing and pray.   Out of such stuff, the stuff the builders of other churches rejected, the Methodists have built a true Church of the People, of the Masses, a church free and unfettered and two-fisted and fighting for nobler houses and mines and men, a church that has forced political tyrants to run for cover and economic empires to change their ways, a church commanding the admira-tion of even its enemies.

They have been guided to two worlds at once, point-ing us to heaven's portal and clearing the way of its stumblingblocks.   If they can but manage to stay at that, our children will grow up in a world a bit more safe and clean and Christian than it was when their renegade fathers first took the Road.

THE DISCIPLES OF CHRIST

CHAPTER XII

THE DISCIPLES OF CHRIST

WHAT we call the Church is a snowball, rolling. It started on "the coasts of Cesarea Philippi," where a disciple was made the rock on which it should be built; it rolled westward, gathering, absorbing, being colored by everything it touched, and coloring everything. It was Hellenized in Greece; Romanized in Rome; it gathered laws, philosophies, thinkers, tinkers, soldiers, saints and devils; it became in time a rolling leviathan of accumulated creeds and catechisms, convictions and conceptions, social custom and economic practice. In shape and size and structure it has changed mightily; yet the gallant core upon which all the rest is built is a simple spiritual ideal. Namely, that men shall seek to gain the mind of Christ within themselves and strive to know the God who made them and all things.

Sometimes, small parts of the snowball have broken off, gone rolling off in independent ways, creating lesser snowballs, other separate churches. A piece broke off in Germany; we call it Lutheranism and it in turn has broken into smaller parts. It broke upon the rocky Alps and we have Calvinism in its many forms. It struck the chalk cliffs of Dover and gave us Methodism and Quakerism and the Baptists and . . . Yet all the while, the first, main, great "snowball," the universal Catholic Church, has rolled on, ahead, beyond us, so that we see it but dimly now, as through a glass. It is an Invisible Church and we are praying we may catch up with it again and gather all our scattered little companies and sects together again. The gathering process we call Church Union.

Now when Thomas Campbell came to America in 1807, he found the Church most shamefully divided against itself. He found Lutherans here and Methodists there, Presbyterians on Main Street and Baptists over the hill, all singing the same hymns and praying the same prayers, each saying to the other, "My way is the right way, my creed the right creed. You must walk my way if you expect to get to Heaven." And with every mile, they broke into more and more sects and more and more. Elias Smith and Abner Jones, both giants in the art of splitting and forming anew, deserted Calvinism in New Hampshire and set up a "Christian Church." James O'Kelley, in Virginia, rebelled against the bishops of Methodism and founded a Republican Methodist Church. Barton W. Stone, Presbyterian, objected to the rigid creed and formalism of his Church, held a famous camp meeting at Cane Ridge, Kentucky, and organized another "Christian" Church, the first church in America with no creed other than the Bible, no name other than Christian. Rebelling was chronic, a habit; perhaps it may all be traced to the political rebelling of 1776.

All this was an old, old story to Thomas Campbell; he may have been disappointed with America, but he could not have been surprised. He was something of a breaker-away himself; he had been a Seceder Presbyterian in County Armaugh, Ireland, whence he came. He knew that his Seceders had broken with the established Church of Scotland; with his own eyes, he had seen them break again into Burghers and Anti-Burghers and yet again into New Lights and Old Lights. Split, split, split. Dissolution, disunion, dissension. It sickened his soul. He may have been glad when his doctor told him to try a sea voyage in 1807. He may have left his divided brethren gladly, hoping for a better church in the new land. Keep this in mind: he did not come to spread his Calvinism, or to build Seceder churches, or any church at all. Thomas Campbell came to America for his health.

But like a sailor rowing a boat on his day off, he drifted down to a Seceder Synod in Philadelphia and asked for a church. He got one, at Washington, in western Pennsylvania. Washington was more of a name than a place; it was the frontier. A sick man, sent to the frontier! It was like throwing a child into deep water and saying to him: "There you are. Sink or swim." That was the choice of every man, woman and child on the frontier of the 1800's. Sink or swim. Fight or die. Shoot first, or be shot yourself. Self preservation came first; certain things, habits, actions, were necessary to life; all else could wait. The frontiersman knew he had to put first things first; he was in a hurry; he took whatever short cuts he could find; he was simple, almost primitive; he shot straight and talked straight; he had little use for anyone who didn't. He was a bit puzzled by the jangling, discordant voices of the disunited churches that followed him to the frontier. Puzzled, when he thought of them at all. Thousands of frontiersmen ignored the Church, laughed at the Bible and knew nothing of God in Christ. (That was not limited to the frontier. Theodore Dwight, president of Yale in 1795, discovered just five church members in his student body; Bishop Meade of Virginia said in 1810 that he expected to find every educated young man he met either a skeptic or an atheist.)

Thomas Campbell looked upon that ludicrous tragedy of division and told the frontier it was all quite unnecessary. Was there not but one God, one Book? Why didn't the churches come together on that and forget the rest, the petty, splitting creeds and theologies they had manufactured themselves? The frontier liked that; it was a short cut, simple, straightforward;

Thomas Campbell was talking their language. He got them, from the start. But the Philadelphia Synod did *not* like it; a Seceder preacher, they thought, should win Seceders, build Seceder churches first and worry about church union afterward. Synod cautioned him and he ignored Synod. When he served a communion in the wilderness, inviting all to come and take it, regardless of creed or sect or anything else, Synod brought him up on charges. It was unorthodox, this "open" communion, irregular; there was no rule for it in the Seceder law-book. Campbell said he couldn't find any law against it in the Bible, so it must be all right. Synod acquitted him, cautioned him, sent him back. But he went back under a shadow. They watched him as a cat watches a mouse, waiting to pounce when he made a mismove, an un-Seceder move. He couldn't stand that. He left them and their Church.

About him he gathered a group of frontier folk; for them, and that the world should know, he drew up a "Declaration and Address" to make their position clear. They were, they said, not another sect, or church; they were the Christian Association of Washington (Pennsylvania); they were a society, a club, like Wesley's Holy Club; they were distinctly not a church, not a denomination; that was the last thing in the world they ever wanted to become. They deplored denominations and the warring of the sects; the Church was "essentially, intentionally, and constitutionally one"; they wanted unity, not division, among the people of God. Unity on the basis of the Bible and Jesus alone, "free from all mixture of human opinions and notions of men." What they wanted was not a reformation, but a *restoration* of the New Testament Church. It was all simple and logical enough, in theory. But in practice . . . well, we shall see.

That was in 1809; when their Association was a year old, they made a gesture of union toward the Presbyterians. The Presbyterians didn't want them; such associations as theirs, said the Calvinists, were a nuisance, promoting "dissension instead of union!" Besides, they erred in doctrine and they outraged church discipline and they did not honor the traditional dignity of a properly ordained and trained ministry; they had laymen preaching! All right, said the Washington Association; if no other church would have them, they'd have their own church. Amazing paradox, this: within two years they were what they had vowed they would never be, a denomination. A tiny denomination of one church and twenty-nine members, but a denomination nevertheless. They were "The First Church of the Christian Association of Washington, Meeting at Cross Roads and Brush Run, Washington County, Pa." A wee church to carry such a name! They had been forced to face the fact, like Jesus and Paul and Luther and Wesley before them, that any truth worth keeping needs an organization to keep it. They elected Thomas Campbell elder, built a meeting house in Brush Run Valley, licensed young Alexander Campbell to preach and served the Lord's Supper every Sabbath Day.

Exit Thomas the father now and enter Alexander the son. Thomas was the innovator, the originator; Alexander was the builder. Like father like son! Alexander had broken, of his own accord, with the Seceders; he could preach and think and write his own thoughts. He brought to the frontier a good education and a rebel's spirit and a faith influenced by two great Christian teachers, John Locke and Johannes Cocceius. Locke had pleaded for Christian unity and tolerance and for the outlawry of creeds; Cocceius had pointed out that there were two covenants instead of one between God and man, one through Adam and one through Christ, and that they were of different value. Alexander Campbell agreed. Equipped with Locke and Cocceius, he leaped into the fray; rushing in where the cautious quailed, he resolutely pushed aside all the old red tape of creed and form and put to the frontier one plain question: What did the New Testament Church require of men for admission to the Church? Only belief in one fact, he said, and submission to one institution. The fact was Jesus Christ the Messiah; the institution was baptism. That was all. He preached that in private houses and in whatever churches he could get in. He preached good Bible sermons, detouring now and then to answer questions. He mentioned the difference between the covenants and he derided the creeds. He went into the question of baptism, read and thought and meditated on it, announced at last that adult immersion was the correct Biblical form. That put him further than ever away from the Presbyterians; it drew him closer to the Baptists. In 1812 he accepted baptism by immersion at the hands of Baptist Elder Luce. When he walked into the Baptist waters, he walked straight into the arms of the Baptist Church, with his family and his Brush Run congregation behind him.

They all joined the Redstone (Pennsylvania) Baptist Association, on condition that they should always be allowed "to teach and preach whatever we learned from the Holy Scriptures, regardless of any human creed." They were Baptists now, not "Campbellites" as the frontier had called them. They remained Baptist for some twenty years. It was a stormy trip.

There were calm seas at first; the straight-from-the-shoulder preaching of Alexander Campbell, plus his belief in immersion, made a sensation in the Baptist camp. They cheered him as he debated the pedobaptists. Twice he did that, once against Seceder John Walker, at Mount Pleasant (!), Ohio, and again against Presbyterian preacher W. L. Maccalla, in Kentucky. He faced

Robert Owen, the social radical and religious skeptic, in a speech that lasted twelve hours and the Baptists said Alexander easily had the best of it, every hour.   But the Baptists were aware, by the time Owen appeared, that some of the Campbell shot was falling into their own camp, on his friends as well as on his enemies.   He is said to have prefaced a speech to a group of Baptist divines with the words: "I have nearly as much against you Baptists as I have against the Presbyterians!"   Alarmed, they watched him; he was playing fast and loose with more than one of their rules and laws and customs and articles of belief; his distinction between the Covenants, his ideas about the administration of baptism and the Supper, his liberal views of church membership and his distaste for the ordained ministry piled up the chips on the blaze until separation was imminent.   The hub of the trouble was that the Baptists were rigid and the Campbellites loose about church ordinances and procedure and their points of agreement were not large enough to outweigh them.   So they left each other and went their separate ways again; once more they were Baptists and Campbellites.

Pause here and consider what had been happening to them.   Started as a protest against sects, they had become a sect themselves.   Offering what seemed to be a simple basis for church union, they had found it to be so complex as to be almost impossible.   (Whenever you get ten men talking about the Bible, you get ten different ideas as to what the Bible is and how it should be interpreted.) Abhorring contention and argument, they had furnished the most ardent debaters and the liveliest arguments of the age. In other words, they were a snowball, rolling, gathering here and rejecting there, changing form and size and character as they went on.

There were twelve thousand Campbellites when the break came with the Baptists in 1830; two years later Barton W. Stone (he of the Cane Ridge camp meeting) marched in with ten thousand more. Other groups came in from all denominations and all directions, but the Stone party, numerically, was the greatest victory. Enough of a victory to make us see that this Church had a dual origin, one at Brush Run and another at Cane Ridge. The Stoneites brought a flare for revivalism and a request that the two groups now be called "The Christian Church," the name they had chosen at Cane Ridge in 1804. Campbell favored "The Disciples of Christ." He had his way; from then on, officially, they are the Disciples of Christ. Legally, however, they have no name; they are only "the Church of Christ at . . ."

Alexander Campbell doubled his efforts as his membership doubled. He never tired of preaching; he had a pen that wouldn't wear out. In a new paper, *The Millennial Harbinger,* he kept up a galling fire of religious discussion; he was particularly effective in his shelling of the clergy of the established churches, calling them scrap doctors and hireling priests, laughing at their clerical collars and their long faces and their claim of a "divine call." He spared them only long enough to found a college, Bethany College in West Virginia. It was a college with a difference, a "college with the Bible for a textbook." He saw to it that the textbook was well studied; he was president of Bethany for twenty years. In that twenty years, he saw his church come up to a membership of two hundred and twenty-five thousand! (For forty years, while the population of the country had been multiplying by three, the Disciples of Christ had been multiplying by sixteen! And this without the help of the waves of foreign immigration which so swelled the ranks of the Lutherans and the Baptists!) He rode out from the campus, now and then, to debate. He met Archbishop Purcell in Cincinnati, on the only occasion in American history when a Roman Catholic leader has been permitted to face a Protestant in public debate. He met N. L. Rice and debated baptism once more, with Henry Clay on the platform as chairman; the argument took sixteen days, eighty-five per cent of it dealt with doctrines and ordinances and both sides said they had won. What the Rice debate did do, of course, was to clarify the position of the Disciples, to point out just where they differed with other Protestants and to give them more of a denominational consciousness than ever.

Social questions began to draw their fire now, as well as theological ones. They were opposed to certain social sins, such as gambling, drinking, card games and the theater, even chess and checkers. They opposed lodges and secret societies, like the Masons and the Odd Fellows; reading novels was a dangerous pastime, smoking was bad in the North but not so bad in the South. They were sure dueling was wrong, not so sure about war. Going to war or refusing to go was an individual matter, for the individual to decide. And then there was slavery, the burning question of the day, the bugaboo of the churches. It never split the Disciples. It was opposed at first by Alexander Campbell, but he and his followers came to argue, by 1845, that slavery was not specifically prohibited by Scripture and was therefore not inconsistent with Christianity. A man could be a good Disciple and a slaveholder at one and the same time. It was another matter for the individual, a matter of "personal opinion." And personal opinions decided the issue for them. Almost equally divided by the Mason and Dixon Line, they followed the opinions, the tides, wherever they were; when war came, they came out on the battlefields and shot at each other; when peace came they went back home and back to church with perfect ease of mind and spirit. They did not divide. They followed the lead of the Episcopalians, walking around the obstacle and meeting again on the other side.

One editor was so jubilant over this that he cried jubilantly: "We can never divide." He spoke too soon. For this "matter-of-opinion" tactic, while it saved them from the war, split them wide open on matters trivial in comparison. With the Civil War safely skirted, they entered on a period of theological pugilism and for a decade their walls were to rock with the shouts of internal strife. It was to be expected. Champions of an ancient book and an ancient church-ideal, they found themselves faced with a world that must have made them feel old indeed. The log cabin was no more; it had grown up into a fine house. Housewives shunned homespun for satins and silk; the men threw away their sickles and scythes for mechanized reapers and binders. There were colleges on the frontiers where the Indians had camped; there were hospitals, theaters, granges, singing-schools and literary societies and a multitude of innovations that bewildered them. The question was: shall the Church keep up with all this, or stand pat? Shall the Disciples adopt the innovations of the hour, or shun them?

There was that particularly noisy innovation, the organ. The Disciples had never had instrumental music in their churches. Should they now? Said one element sharply, "No. The Bible says nothing of organs!" Said another element: "Why not? We have melodeons in our parlors. If the organ will help make the service beautiful . . . ?" Churches split over it; churches were almost wrecked. At last, it was decided that each church was to settle the question for itself. Which each church had been doing, anyway!

There was trouble over the Supper. Should the unimmersed be served the Lord's Supper, or only the immersed? Should *all* come, or only the chosen few? Open communion, or closed? It ended with the declaration that they would "neither invite nor exclude," which was sensible. Few Disciples today care to talk about it; few of them know anything but open communion.

They quarreled over whether or not they should call their preachers "Reverend so-and-so," (historically, there has been almost no distinction between pastors and elders) and whether they should supplant the old rulership of lay elders by "one-man rule," or rule by a pastor. This was a sham battle, too; it ended with the progressives having "pastors" and the conservatives having preaching elders whom they refused to call pastors and with the use of "Reverend" still unsettled.

But the great decisive battle of the pugilistic era was the struggle over the missionary societies. Back in 1849 they had created a short-lived "American Christian Missionary Society" which had sent one missionary to Jerusalem and another to Africa, both of whom failed quickly. There was opposition to that Society; many who had been anti-organists now became anti-missionary society, claiming that it was wrong to set up any society larger than the local church; they were, they held, "restorers of an ancient order," a Biblical order, and there had been no such missionary societies in the Bible. They objected not to missionary work, but to missionary *societies*. Their opponents saw no way of doing effective missionary work abroad without the aid of a strong organization at home. It was an impasse, a hurdle hard to get over. Compromises were attempted, and failed. The conservative, anti-society group withdrew from the Disciples of Christ and formed their own church, the "Churches of Christ"; in 1934, they had 433,714 members. It was the worst blow the Disciples were ever to take. But perhaps it was best. It gave the Disciples a free hand to proceed as they wished and they were saved from a crueler blow. They were saved from becoming legalists, from becoming mere proponents of a form at the cost of the Spirit. And it was the beginning of a change of mind within their membership, a change from the old desire to restore a pattern of church organization, to an insistence on the gaining and spreading of the Will and Spirit behind the pattern. The only bright spot in this whole period was the writing of a "Synopsis" of the Disciples' position, by Isaac Errett. Errett cleared the air by calling them back to the fundamentals upon which they had been founded and by calling them back to the Book and the Christ they had almost lost in their quarreling. And he cleared the way for future understanding and progress.

The sun broke through their dark clouds of dispute in 1875; they moved west as their frontier receded, following the tide to Oregon and California. These were the boom days of Church as well as State; the Disciples gained, in this westward push, their greatest strength. They remained, however, what they had always been, a frontier church; by 1890 they were over a million strong and seventy-three per cent rural. Only six per cent plus lived in the city.

They greeted the new frontier with a rebirth of energy in all directions. There was a rebirth in journalism. Now journalism, to them, had always been a forte; lacking bishops, they had placed their greatest power in the hands of their editors, who in turn have produced a succession of brilliant papers, not the least of which is *The Christian Century* of today. The *Century* exemplifies their newer journalism: it is free, fearless, nonsectarian, liberal and read by every denomination in America.

There was a rebirth of missionary effort. The ladies started that by starting a "Women's Board of Missions" in 1874. Stung by the taunt of an editor who told them bluntly that their Church was "the only people not obeying the Great Commission and not even trying to," the Disciples en masse threw their efforts and their resources into the task of preaching the Gospel to every creature and forgot completely their old and useless squabble over missionary "societies." Souls mattered now, not forms. They sought souls for Christ first in Europe, then in India, China, Japan and the Belgian Congo. Inspired by success in this effort, they actually set up a Board of Church Extension and a Board of Ministerial Relief! In other words, they had adjusted themselves to a growing church in a growing world.

In the old days they had been suspicious of denominational education; a writer had written: "If the union of God's people is the desirable thing, then let us pray, O Lord, take away all denominational colleges, and give us no more forever." But now the presence of a young army of youth in their great membership, demanding education, made them think differently. This youth would be educated, somewhere. It might be well to educate them in their own colleges. So they built their own colleges. They built Drake, Hiram, Texas Christian, Transylvania, Phillips, Cotner and Virginia Christian. They created "Bible chairs," or professorships, at Michigan and Virginia; they have "affiliated" theological schools, for the training of their young ministers, at the Universities of Chicago, Missouri, Oregon and California.

The old evangelistic passion appeared in modern dress; evangelistic "teams" and "companies" and "mass meetings" and high-pressure methods (borrowed from business) brought them one hundred thousand new members in five years. (They spent the next five in separating the wheat from the chaff and dropped a cool two hundred thousand!) And the old passion for co-operation and reunion among the churches took a new lease on life. The Disciples joined the Federal Council and led in the forming of a "Committee on Co-operation in Latin America" on the missions field. They moved toward reunion with the Congregationalists and the Baptists. Our generation should see them merge with the Baptists; they have much in common and the few differences which separate them are trivial. But they dare to look for more than just this combination. They still hope that *all* the Church may again be one. Here is the late Peter Ainslee, one of their finest prophets, speaking his mind on the subject: "In this new day, with its new vocabulary, new idealism and new hope, there must come a Christian revolution—not violent, like the American or French revolutions, but as gently as the flowing tides and blooming flowers. It must come with such force that the present inequalities of Christendom shall be wiped out. Let the episcopal bodies hold to the Episcopacy. . . . Let those bodies that hold to baptism by immersion still practice what they believe. . . . Let the creedal bodies hold to their creeds. . . . But let them abandon denominationalizing as one of the things for which they stand."

Crucial questions have faced them in our own times. There came the question of open or closed membership; should they admit only the immersed, the baptized, to membership, or should the gates be thrown open to all who sincerely loved the Lord?   It was perhaps the most perilous question they had ever faced; the form of baptism almost became a dogma, the very thing Alexander Campbell had fought so hard, and it nearly undid them, nearly cheated them of their great reunion-izing opportunity.   At last they settled it in good Dis-ciples fashion: they left it for the churches to decide. Some of their modern churches require baptism before membership and some require only a simple confession of Christ.   Should they have a great ruling national body, or Convention, like the Methodist General Con-ference or the Presbyterian Assembly?   No, they de-cided, they would not have that.   Ultra-democratic, their national convention is no more than a mass meeting, provided not for laws and discipline, but for discussion and fellowship.   Should they accept or reject the new "higher criticism of the Bible" and take sides in the Fundamentalist-Modernist controversy?   No, they would not; the Disciples have had few heresy trials; they left the way open for champions of both causes in their pulpits.   Honor them for this: they could produce an Alexander Campbell and a Barton Stone in one century, a Peter Ainslee and a *Christian Century* in the next.

Should they preach that most recent innovation, the "social gospel"? Some do and some don't.

An American church, a strictly *native* church, these Disciples of Christ.   Born on our own American frontier, they developed with it, having at first all its simple homespun virtues, interests and attitudes, but changing them to more sophisticated ones as the frontier changed its virtues, attitudes and interests and became more urbanized.   They have not only been influenced by us; they have influenced us.   They have simplified our thinking on religion, cutting away the mass and dross of confusing creed and putting in its place a simple confession of Christ.   They have proved that a great and powerful Protestant Church (they stand sixth in the United States) can be built without a creed and maintained without one.   They have set the pace for Bible study, a pace set for them when Alexander Campbell pointed out the relative values of Old and New Testaments and thereby anticipated the modern view of the Scriptures.   They were launched in fine fervor against a great evil: the evil of the sect.   At first they suggested that the imposition of an ancient pattern, a New Testament pattern, might overcome that evil; now they are suggesting that the gaining of the mind, the tolerant, loving, all-inclusive, creed-leaping mind which was in Christ, is the only chance, the only foundation for the unity of the worshipers of the God who was in Christ.

When we know fully what they mean by that, we shall have a better right to sing triumphantly the marching song of the Church:

> "Like a mighty army
>   Moves the church of God;
> . . . We are not divided,
>   All one body we."

THE END